Lindt

COOKBOOK

COOKBOOK

60 delicious recipes using the finest
Lindt chocolate

EBURY
PRESS

CONTENTS

FAMILY 86

HOSTING 106

FESTIVE 128

THE LINDT HISTORY

An entrepreneurial spirit. A chocolate revolution.
The perfect partnership. This is the story of how
Lindt & Sprüngli came to be.

1800s

Pioneers in chocolate

It all began with the opening of David Sprüngli's small confectionery in Zurich. The business grew quickly thanks to Sprüngli's entrepreneurial spirit and passion for chocolate. Sprüngli soon became renowned among chocolate manufacturers.

1845

Early success

In a small confectionery shop in Marktgasse, in Zurich's old town, David Sprüngli and his son, Rudolf Sprüngli-Ammann, produced the first solid bar of chocolate in the German-speaking part of Switzerland. It instantly became a success.

Opposite right: Lindt conche machine.

1847

First chocolate factory

Sprüngli grew rapidly, opening the Schleifetobel factory in Horgen in 1847. You could smell chocolate in the air when production began.

1859

A novel pâtisserie

David Sprüngli and son inaugurated a second confectionery on Paradeplatz – the, until now, famous Confiserie Sprüngli. Its elegant interiors quickly found favour among the locals, making it a popular place to get together.

CHOCOLATE ENTREPRENEURS

1879

The invention of conching

Meanwhile, in Berne, Rodolphe Lindt, the son of a pharmacist, had just started a small confectionery. Shortly after opening in 1879, Lindt's chocolate company Rod. Lindt & Sons only produced hard, bitter chocolate – just like other chocolatiers at that time. Undeterred, Lindt kept experimenting, until one Friday night after months of testing, he left his factory without turning off the conching machine. It churned all night and all through the weekend.

The chocolate Lindt found on Monday was delicately smooth and tasted like it never had before. Chocolate had changed forever. That was the beginning of incomparably delicate, world-renowned, Lindt chocolate fondant.

The secret to his chocolate was all in the conching process he had invented, which created a fine-melting texture by evenly combining the cocoa mass and cocoa butter with other ingredients like sugar and milk for a prolonged period of time. Lindt's conching technique created a 'melting chocolate' so fine and flavourful it was impossible to resist. This was the start of a chocolate revolution. Lindt kept his invention top secret until the Sprünglis came into the picture. Today, conching is used by chocolate manufacturers all over the world.

THE BEGINNING OF LINDT & SPRÜNGLI

1899

The perfect partnership

When, in 1879, Lindt happened upon the secret that would effectively put Switzerland on the map as a top-tier chocolate manufacturer, Johann Rudolf Sprüngli took notice. His interest had been piqued; he recognised a fellow chocolate connoisseur.

But it wasn't until 1899 that the two entrepreneurs met. Johann Rudolf Sprüngli had just completed construction on a larger factory in Kilchberg-Bendlikon, the location of today's headquarters, to increase output. In Berne, the high demand for Rodolphe Lindt's creamy chocolate was beginning to strain Lindt's small, antiquated production facilities. So when Johann Rudolf Sprüngli offered to buy the company for an impressive 1.5 million gold francs – including the brand Lindt and the secret recipe – Lindt agreed under the condition that he still had a say in the business. The perfect partnership was born, and continued until Sprüngli fully ran the business.

1892

How Sprüngli became Lindt & Sprüngli

When Rudolf Sprüngli-Ammann stepped down in 1892, he divided the company between his two sons, Johann Rudolf Sprüngli-Schifferli and David Robert Sprüngli-Baud. Johann Rudolf took over the factory in Horgen, later to be part of Lindt & Sprüngli, while his younger brother received the two confectionery stores in Zurich.

Above left: Rodolphe Lindt, 1900.

Above right: Lindt factory in Kilchberg, Switzerland, 1898.

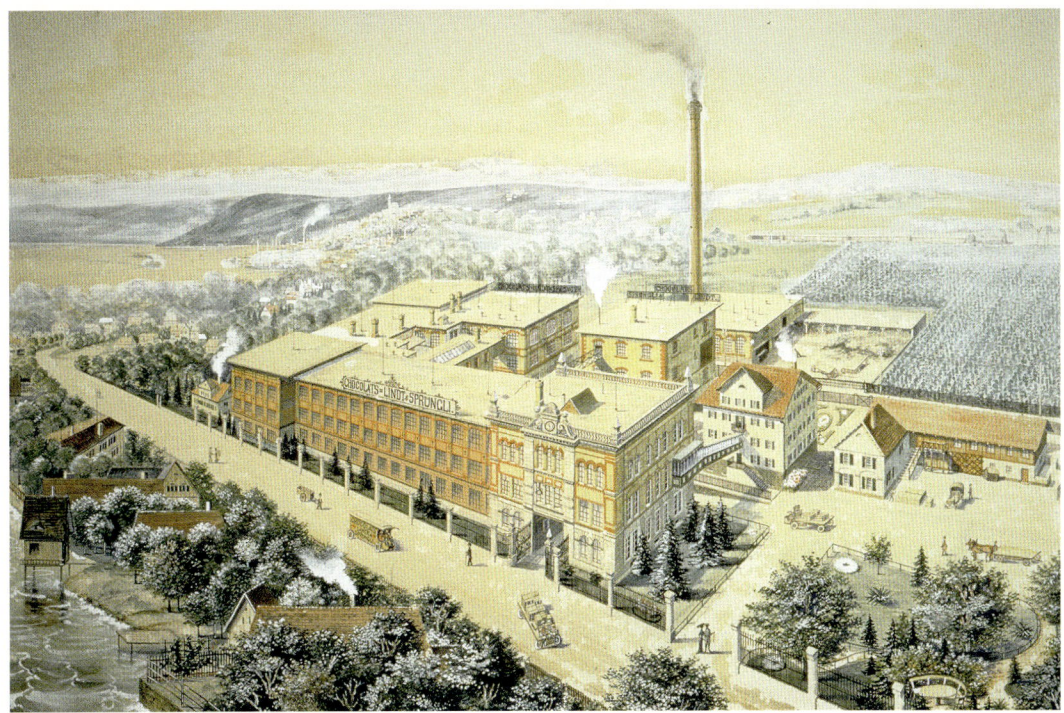

1900s

Start of the century

The new century started off strong for Lindt & Sprüngli, though it was not without its challenges. Despite the First World War, the Swiss chocolate industry flourished, with Lindt & Sprüngli playing a significant part in its success. By 1915, the majority of the output was exported abroad. Even during the Second World War, Lindt & Sprüngli did not sacrifice its dedication to quality. At the end of the war – coincidentally the 100-year anniversary of Lindt & Sprüngli – sales rose rapidly again.

1920s

Growth abroad

At the beginning of the twentieth century, Lindt & Sprüngli established general agencies and subsidiaries in Germany, the US and the UK. In 1930, the company's name was changed to today's name, 'Chocoladefabriken Lindt & Sprüngli AG'.

International expansion

The company continued to grow in all key markets, with subsidiaries and distributor businesses. Today, Lindt & Sprüngli is number 1 in the global premium chocolate market and we are well-known for our chocolate classics.

1932

Bâtons Kirsch

The year 1932 saw the launch of a true Swiss original, the 'Bâtons Kirsch', which proved to be a real success for Lindt & Sprüngli.

1945

100 years of Lindt & Sprüngli

Lindt & Sprüngli turned 100 and celebrated the big anniversary with a 12-part advertising series. The anniversary coincided with the end of the Second World War, and chocolate consumption picked up again.

1949

Chocolate gold – LINDOR

The Lindt Master Chocolatiers wanted to create something heavenly to lift customers' spirits after the war, so they set to work experimenting with chocolate recipes until, in 1949, they came across a chocolate so luxuriously smooth it could be compared to melted gold. It was named LINDOR. LINDOR combines the French word for 'gold' ('or') with 'Lindt'. First appearing as a chocolate bar with a delicately melting filling, LINDOR was only associated with the signature truffles 20 years later.

1952

A hoppy surprise – the Lindt GOLD BUNNY

In 1952, the Lindt GOLD BUNNY first appeared. Inspired by his daughter, a Lindt Master Chocolatier created a bunny out of the finest Swiss chocolate. He lovingly wrapped it in gold foil to make it shine and tied it with a red-ribbon bow and a little bell so it would never get lost. Today, the Lindt GOLD BUNNY is an Easter staple, signalling that spring is just around the corner.

1969

A worldwide favourite – LINDOR Truffles

Finally, in 1969, Lindt & Sprüngli released the first LINDOR Truffles as a Christmas specialty. They became an immediate success and customers were sad to see them go when the festive season was over. They were so sorely missed that we soon made them a permanent part of our chocolate range. They quickly became a Lindt staple and global chocolate phenomenon.

1979

Chocolate classics

Before the end of the decade, in 1979, Lindt's premium collection CONNAISSEURS pralines were created for special gifting occasions and expanded into their own brand line.

1989

EXCELLENCE

In 1989, yet another classic was created. Lindt & Sprüngli introduced the extra-thin EXCELLENCE Dark Chocolate Bars, with intense and elegant flavours and a fine texture.

2000s: THE FUTURE OF LINDT & SPRÜNGLI

Lindt & Sprüngli is committed to creating fresh new flavours that inspire consumers while maintaining the highest quality in every product. The turn of the century saw a wealth of new, delicious chocolate creations and exciting initiatives that continue to bring the world of Lindt closer to you.

2008

Lindt & Sprüngli Farming Program

Sustainability is an integral part of Lindt & Sprüngli's corporate philosophy and is firmly anchored in our strategy, from the sourcing of the cocoa beans to the finished chocolate product. Since 2008, the Lindt & Sprüngli Farming Program has been an expression of this commitment to sustainability.

2009

An exciting year

Swiss global tennis champion Roger Federer became brand ambassador for Lindt in 2009. In the same year, Lindt & Sprüngli founded its own global retail network, creating a premium chocolate experience for the world.

2011

Lindt Christmas magic

The Lindt TEDDY launched in time to bring some extra magic during the festive season in 2011.

2013

Giving back

In 2013, Lindt & Sprüngli founded the Lindt Cocoa Foundation and the Lindt Chocolate Competence Foundation. The Lindt Cocoa Foundation improves the social and ecological environment around chocolate production. Fostering sustainable agriculture, the Lindt Cocoa Foundation supplements existing efforts designed to improve the living and working conditions of the cocoa farmers. While the charitable Lindt Chocolate Competence Foundation aims to sustain, cultivate and promote Switzerland's long-term standing as a business location for chocolate and further strengthen the Swiss chocolate-making expertise.

THE LINDT DIFFERENCE

What makes Lindt chocolate so exceptional?

The finest cocoa

The foundation for the incomparable Lindt taste comes from the careful selection, in-house processing and blending of high quality beans from the world's most renowned origins. Committed to sustainability, the dedicated Lindt & Sprüngli Farming Program supports cocoa farmers and their communities.

Unique roasting and grinding

A unique process perfected over decades, the Lindt Master Chocolatiers roast the beans for optimum flavour and grind them extremely fine - essential for the remarkable melting taste of Lindt.

The Lindt invention

In 1879, Rodolphe Lindt revolutionised chocolate making with 'conching' - the intense mixing of heated liquid chocolate to create the silky smooth Lindt chocolate texture.

The best ingredients

The Lindt Master Chocolatiers rigorously select and process only the most premium ingredients from world renowned growing regions. For example, to maintain the delicious roasting aroma, nuts are roasted in-house and freshly worked into the chocolate.

Finishing with perfection

With attention to detail, the Lindt Master Chocolatiers place the finishing touches on their masterpieces, lovingly decorating and wrapping them in exquisite packaging.

Driven by their passion, dedication and innovative spirit since 1845, the Lindt Master Chocolatiers create the ultimate Lindt chocolate delights.

CLASSICS

DARK CHOCOLATE SHORTBREAD

Shortbread: a beautifully buttery Scottish biscuit. Our Lindt Master Chocolatiers have sprinkled this classic with a little Lindt magic with our EXCELLENCE 70% Dark Chocolate…

MAKES: 24
PREP: 35 mins + chilling
COOK: 15 mins

200g unsalted butter,
  at room temperature
100g soft light brown sugar
½ tsp vanilla extract
315g plain flour, plus extra
  for dusting
24 squares **Lindt
  EXCELLENCE 70%
  Dark Chocolate** (250g)
  (see Tip)
Sea salt flakes, for
  sprinkling

1. Preheat the oven to 160°C/140°C Fan/Gas 3. Line 2 large, flat baking sheets with greaseproof paper.

2. Using an electric mixer, cream together the butter, sugar and vanilla extract until pale and fluffy.

3. Mix in the flour in 4 batches until all has been incorporated and you have a smooth dough.

4. Wrap the dough in cling film and chill in the fridge for 10 minutes.

5. Lightly dust a work surface with flour and roll out the dough to 1cm thick.

6. Cut into 24 rectangles that are 4 x 5cm, big enough to fit a square of the Lindt chocolate. Using a spatula or palette knife, carefully transfer the shortbread rectangles to the prepared baking sheets, well spaced (2.5cm) apart. Top each with a square of EXCELLENCE 70% Dark Chocolate and press into the dough slightly.

7. Bake for 12-15 minutes or until the shortbreads are golden. You may need to make them in batches.

8. Cool for 2 minutes on the baking sheets before sprinkling lightly with sea salt flakes. Leave to cool completely on the baking sheets before transferring to airtight storage containers. These will keep for up to 4 days at room temperature.

CHOCOLATIER'S TIP
Many flavours of Lindt EXCELLENCE work as substitutions for the EXCELLENCE 70% Dark Chocolate used here. Try our EXCELLENCE Orange Intense for a zesty twist, or go refreshing with Mint Intense.

ULTIMATE CHOCOLATE BROWNIES

This is the epitome of brownie brilliance – our Lindt Master
Chocolatiers have tested countless combinations of our luxurious
EXCELLENCE chocolates to create this rich, indulgent and fabulously
fudgy masterpiece. Get ready for a slice of chocolate heaven...

MAKES: 9–12
PREP: 20 mins + cooling
COOK: 30 mins

200g unsalted butter,
  roughly chopped, plus
  extra for greasing
200g **Lindt EXCELLENCE
  70% Dark Chocolate**,
  finely chopped
3 large eggs
275g light brown sugar
1 tsp vanilla extract
90g plain flour
40g cocoa powder
35g ground almonds
75g **Lindt EXCELLENCE
  85% Dark Chocolate**,
  roughly chopped
50g **Lindt EXCELLENCE
  Extra Creamy Milk
  Chocolate**, chopped

1. Preheat the oven to 180°C/160°C Fan/Gas 4. Grease and line a
   20cm square tin with greaseproof paper.

2. Put the butter and chopped 70% Dark Chocolate into a heatproof
   bowl set over a pan of barely simmering water, ensuring the bottom
   of the bowl doesn't come into contact with the water, then stir until
   melted. Alternatively, pop into a microwave-safe bowl and melt in
   30-second bursts, stirring between each. Remove from the heat
   and leave to cool.

3. Whisk together the eggs, sugar and vanilla extract with an electric
   whisk until light and fluffy.

4. Fold into the melted chocolate mix, followed by the flour, cocoa
   powder and ground almonds. Mix until you have a smooth batter.

5. Stir in the chopped Lindt EXCELLENCE 85% Dark Chocolate until
   evenly distributed throughout the batter.

CHOCOLATIER'S TIP
This recipe is designed to produce a fudgy brownie, so it is key not to
over-bake. Therefore, make sure you remove the brownies from the
oven while there is still a wobble in the centre.

TO DECORATE
(OPTIONAL):
100g **Lindt EXCELLENCE
Extra Creamy Milk
Chocolate**, finely
chopped

6. Carefully pour into the prepared tin. Sprinkle over the chopped EXCELLENCE Extra Creamy Milk Chocolate pieces. Bake for 25–30 minutes, or until the top is firm but there is a slight wobble in the centre. Leave to cool before removing from the tin.

7. For a final flourish (if using), put the chopped Lindt EXCELLENCE Extra Creamy Milk Chocolate into a heatproof bowl set over a pan of barely simmering water, ensuring the bottom of the bowl doesn't come into contact with the water. Stir until melted, smooth and glossy. Alternatively, pop into a microwave-safe bowl and melt in 30-second bursts, stirring between each. Drizzle over the cooled brownies and leave to cool completely before slicing.

PEAR AND CHOCOLATE CRUMBLE

Our Lindt Master Chocolatiers have added a little Lindt magic to the classic English crumble. Simply serve warm with melting vanilla ice cream and our intense EXCELLENCE 70% Dark Chocolate.

SERVES: 6
PREP: 30 mins
COOK: 50 mins

FOR THE CRUMBLE:
200g cold butter, diced, plus extra for greasing
250g plain flour
45g jumbo rolled oats (see Tip)
Pinch of salt
100g demerara sugar

FOR THE PEARS:
6 pears, cored, peeled and roughly chopped
50g soft light brown sugar, or to taste
1 tbsp plain flour
1 tsp ground cinnamon (see Tip)
100g **Lindt EXCELLENCE 70% Dark Chocolate**, finely chopped

TO SERVE:
Good-quality vanilla ice cream
100g **Lindt EXCELLENCE 70% Dark Chocolate**, cut along the squares

1. Preheat the oven to 180°C/160°C Fan/Gas 4. Grease a 24cm ovenproof baking dish with a little butter.

2. To make the crumble, tip the flour into a large mixing bowl and rub in the butter until the mixture resembles breadcrumbs. Add the rolled oats, salt and demerara sugar. Mix well and set aside.

3. For the pears: tip the pears into the prepared ovenproof dish (ours was around 18 x 26 x 6cm) and mix with the sugar, flour, cinnamon and chopped chocolate. Stir to coat then flatten into an even layer. Sprinkle the crumble mixture over the fruit.

4. Bake for 40–50 minutes or until the pears are soft and the top is golden brown and crisp (but not burnt).

5. Once cooked, remove from the oven and divide into 6 portions. Serve with a scoop of vanilla ice cream and a diamond of Lindt EXCELLENCE 70% Dark Chocolate.

CHOCOLATIER'S TIP
Ring the changes with your crumble topping by swapping the oats for roughly chopped almonds for a bit of a crunch. You can also swap the ground cinnamon for ground ginger, if you prefer.

CHOCOLATE BANANA BREAD

Our Lindt Master Chocolatiers love baking banana bread to make the most of overripe bananas and minimise food waste. As expected, they couldn't help adding a luxurious Lindt twist with our intense EXCELLENCE 70% Dark Chocolate and an indulgent chocolate ganache. Delicious for breakfast, as a sweet snack or as a dessert.

MAKES: 1 loaf
PREP: 20 mins + cooling
COOK: 1 hour

115g unsalted butter,
 melted and cooled,
 plus extra for greasing
150g plain flour
4 tbsp cocoa powder
1 tsp baking powder
½ tsp bicarbonate of soda
Pinch of salt
170g golden caster sugar
2 large eggs
300g ripe mashed bananas
 (about 3–4 bananas)
180ml plain yogurt
1 tsp vanilla extract
100g **Lindt EXCELLENCE
 70% Dark Chocolate**,
 roughly chopped
 (see Tip)

FOR THE CHOCOLATE
 GANACHE:
150g **Lindt EXCELLENCE
 70% Dark Chocolate**,
 roughly chopped
180ml double cream
15g unsalted butter,
 roughly chopped

1. Preheat the oven to 180°C/160°C Fan/Gas 4. Grease and line a 900g (2lb) loaf tin with greaseproof paper.

2. In a medium bowl, sift together the flour with the cocoa powder, baking powder, bicarbonate of soda and salt. Set aside.

3. Beat together the sugar and melted butter until well combined. Add the eggs, one at a time, mixing well after each addition. Beat in the mashed bananas, yogurt and vanilla extract and mix well.

4. Add the flour mixture and mix until just combined. Mix in the chopped chocolate until evenly distributed throughout the batter.

5. Pour into the prepared tin and smooth over the top. Bake in the centre of the oven for 50 minutes–1 hour or until a skewer inserted into the centre of the cake comes out clean. Check on the cake towards the end of the cooking time, and if the top is browning before the loaf is cooked, cover it with some tin foil. Leave to cool in the tin for 10 minutes before turning out onto a wire rack to finish cooling completely.

6. To make the ganache, put the chopped chocolate in a medium heatproof bowl and set aside.

7. Pour the cream into a saucepan and gently bring to a simmer. Remove from the heat and pour it over the chopped chocolate. Add the butter and stir until both the butter and chocolate are melted into a smooth and glossy ganache.

8. Leave to cool until thick enough to spread over the cooled loaf.

CHOCOLATIER'S TIP
Swap the chopped dark chocolate for our EXCELLENCE White Chocolate with a Touch of Vanilla for a sweeter note.

ULTIMATE CHOCOLATE FONDUE

Get set for the ultimate chocolate experience with our gloriously gooey chocolate fondue made with a combination of our rich and decadent EXCELLENCE 78% Dark Chocolate and luxuriously smooth EXCELLENCE Extra Creamy Milk Chocolate. Perfect for adding a little fun to your dinner party or for sharing with friends and family during a cosy night in...

SERVES: 10–12
PREP: 5 mins
COOK: 10 mins

FOR THE FONDUE:
300g **Lindt EXCELLENCE 78% Dark Chocolate**, chopped
300g **Lindt EXCELLENCE Extra Creamy Milk Chocolate**, chopped
415ml double cream

FOR DIPPING (SEE TIP):
Marzipan, sliced into rounds
Clementines and oranges, peeled and separated into segments
Physalis, leaves removed

1. Put both chopped chocolates into a medium heatproof bowl and set aside.

2. Pour the cream into a medium saucepan and bring to a simmer, stirring often to ensure it does not overflow.

3. Pour the cream over the chocolate and leave to stand for 2 minutes – the chocolate will start to melt.

4. Mix with a spatula until smooth and glossy.

5. Pour into a fondue pot set over a low heat and serve with slices of marzipan and your chosen fruits.

CHOCOLATIER'S TIP
Alter your dipping fruits depending on the time of year for a sumptuous and seasonal dessert.

CHOCOLATE TORTE

Master this beautifully light chocolate torte made using our rich and intense EXCELLENCE 85% Dark Chocolate and a hint of vanilla for sweetness. The perfect gluten-free dinner party dessert served with a spoonful of whipped cream and fresh berries.

SERVES: 8–10
PREP: 25 mins
COOK: 1 hour

345g unsalted butter at room temperature, diced, plus extra for greasing
400g **Lindt EXCELLENCE 85% Dark Chocolate**, chopped
200g caster sugar
100g ground almonds
2 tsp vanilla extract
6 large eggs, separated
Pinch of salt

TO DECORATE:
Icing sugar
Whipped cream
Fresh berries

1. Preheat the oven to 150°C/130°C Fan/Gas 2. Grease and line the base and sides of a 23cm round loose-bottomed sandwich tin with baking paper. Set on a baking sheet.

2. Put the butter and chopped chocolate into a heatproof bowl set over a pan of barely simmering water, ensuring the bottom of the bowl doesn't come into contact with the water. Melt the butter and chocolate, stirring often. Alternatively, pop both into a microwave-safe bowl and melt in 30-second bursts, stirring between each, until smooth.

3. Remove from the heat and whisk in the sugar, almonds and vanilla extract until smooth. Whisk in the egg yolks.

4. Using an electric whisk, in a clean mixing bowl whisk the egg whites with the salt until stiff peaks form.

5. Carefully fold the egg whites, one-third at a time, into the chocolate mixture. Take care not to overmix, as you want to keep in as much air as possible.

6. Spoon into the prepared tin and smooth the top.

7. Bake for 1 hour, or until the edge has set and the middle has risen and cracked slightly. Leave to cool completely in the tin.

8. When completely cool, remove from the tin and set onto a flat plate. Decorate with a stencil and icing sugar to create a decorative pattern. Serve slices with whipped cream and fresh berries.

CHOCOLATIER'S TIP
For a more decadent taste, add a hint of coffee to bring out the flavours of the chocolate. You can also add a squeeze of orange juice for a child-friendly alternative.

DOUBLE CHOCOLATE DIPPED STRAWBERRIES

Plump, ripe and juicy strawberries coated in our luxurious
Swiss chocolate – our Lindt Master Chocolatiers' favourite way
to reach their 5-a-day…

MAKES: 12–14
PREP: 15 mins + chilling

12–14 large, ripe
   strawberries
300g **Lindt EXCELLENCE**
   70% Dark Chocolate,
   chopped
50g **Lindt EXCELLENCE**
   White Chocolate with
   a Touch of Vanilla, or
   Lindt COOKING 70%
   Dark Intense, chopped

1. Wipe the strawberries with a damp cloth and pat dry. Do not wash them. Line a large baking sheet with greaseproof paper.

2. Pop the chopped Lindt EXCELLENCE 70% Dark Chocolate or Lindt COOKING 70% Dark Intense into a heatproof bowl set over a pan of barely simmering water, ensuring the bottom of the bowl doesn't come into contact with the water, then stir until melted. Alternatively, pop the chocolate into a microwave-safe bowl and melt in 30-second bursts, stirring between each. Remove from the heat and leave to cool.

3. Hold a strawberry by its green stem and carefully dip into the melted dark chocolate. Carefully shake off the excess and place the chocolate-dipped strawberry onto the baking sheet. Repeat with the remaining strawberries.

4. Place the baking sheet into the fridge for about 5 minutes, or until the chocolate coating has just set.

5. Meanwhile, melt the chopped Lindt EXCELLENCE White Chocolate with a Touch of Vanilla as in step 2 and spoon into a disposable piping bag. Snip a very small tip out of the bag.

6. Remove the dipped strawberries from the fridge and pipe contrasting chocolate drizzles onto the dark chocolate coating. Return to the baking sheet and leave to set in the fridge for 20 minutes.

CHOCOLATIER'S TIP
You can use this technique with a variety of fresh fruits slotted onto wooden skewers; try using bite-sized pieces of kiwi, melon or pineapple for a tropical twist. To make these dairy-free and vegan-friendly, simply omit the white chocolate drizzle.

LINDOR ULTIMATE CHOCOLATE CAKE

Every baker should have a go-to chocolate cake in their recipe repertoire for special occasions. This rich and indulgent cake is magnificently moist thanks to the addition of the buttermilk and smooth, melted dark chocolate. Dare we say this is the ultimate chocolate cake?

SERVES: 8–10
PREP: 45 mins + cooling and chilling
COOK: 35 mins

175g unsalted butter, at room temperature, plus extra to grease
250g plain flour
25g cocoa powder
1¾ tsp bicarbonate of soda
1 tsp baking powder
1 tsp salt
220g dark brown sugar
100g caster sugar
100g **Lindt EXCELLENCE 90% Dark Chocolate**, melted and cooled
2 large eggs
2 tsp vanilla extract
350ml buttermilk

Ingredients continued overleaf →

1. Preheat the oven to 180°C/160°C Fan/Gas 4. Grease and line three 23cm, round loose-bottomed sandwich tins with baking paper.

2. In a medium bowl, sift the flour with the cocoa powder, bicarbonate of soda, baking powder and salt and set aside.

3. In the bowl of a stand mixer fitted with the paddle attachment, beat the sugars with the butter on medium-high for about 1 minute until light and fluffy (you could do this by hand but it will take a little longer).

4. Reduce the speed to medium-low and pour in the melted chocolate in a slow and steady stream. Mix until combined.

5. Add the eggs, one at a time, and beat until just combined. Add the vanilla extract.

6. Add the dry flour mix into the butter mixture in 3 parts, alternating with buttermilk in 2 parts, beating well between each addition.

7. Divide the batter evenly between the tins and smooth over the tops.

8. Bake in the centre of the oven for 25–35 minutes or until a skewer inserted into the centre of the cakes comes out clean.

9. Leave to cool in the tins for 10 minutes before removing from the tins and transferring to wire racks to finish cooling completely.

Method continued overleaf →

LINDOR ULTIMATE CHOCOLATE CAKE *continued*

FOR THE DARK CHOCOLATE
   BUTTERCREAM:
500g unsalted butter,
   at room temperature
200g icing sugar
225g **Lindt EXCELLENCE
   70% Dark Chocolate**,
   or **Lindt COOKING
   70% Dark Intense**,
   melted and cooled
2 tsp vanilla extract

TO DECORATE:
60 **LINDOR Chocolate
   Truffles** (you can use
   3 different types –
   milk, dark and white),
   unwrapped
Edible gold leaf

10. Individually wrap each cake in cling film and chill in the fridge for at least 2 hours.

11. Meanwhile, to make the buttercream, in the bowl of a stand mixer fitted with the paddle attachment, beat the butter with the icing sugar for about a minute on medium speed until combined. Reduce the speed to medium-low and stream in the melted chocolate until combined. Add the vanilla extract, increase the speed to medium-high and beat for 5 minutes or until very light and fluffy (you could do this by hand but it will take much longer).

12. To assemble the cake, remove the 3 cakes from the fridge and set onto a flat board. Trim (if needed) to ensure they are smooth and flat.

13. Place 1 cake onto a cake stand or flat plate and spread with a layer of the buttercream. Lay another cake on top. Repeat, spreading and layering before lightly icing the sides and top of the cake to crumb coat. Chill in the freezer for 30 minutes, or 3 hours in the fridge. Once the first layer of icing is set, spread the remaining icing onto the cake and smooth with a palette knife. Gently arrange the LINDOR Truffles around the top and bottom ring of the cake. Finish by placing a few flecks of the gold leaf onto the sides and top of the cake – this is most easily done using a small paintbrush.

CHOCOLATIER'S TIP
Get creative with the cake decorations; try using our subtly sweet EXCELLENCE White Chocolate with a Touch of Vanilla to make contrasting curls, arrange pieces of fresh fruit on top – raspberries and sliced strawberries work well and cut through the richness of the cake.

LINDOR HOT CHOCOLATE

Nothing beats coming in from a chilly day to a mug of steaming hot chocolate. Add a little luxury to this winter ritual by using our smooth and creamy LINDOR Truffles and our EXCELLENCE 65% Milk Chocolate.

MAKES: 1 mug
PREP: 5 mins
COOK: 5 mins

200ml milk
30ml double cream
4 **LINDOR Milk Truffles**,
   unwrapped and
   chopped (see Tip)
20g **Lindt EXCELLENCE**
   Extra Creamy Milk
   Chocolate, chopped

TO DECORATE:
Whipped cream
Lindt EXCELLENCE
   70% Dark Chocolate,
   melted
Lindt EXCELLENCE
   70% Dark Chocolate,
   grated into shavings

1. Pour the milk and cream into a medium-sized saucepan and slowly bring to a simmer.

2. Add the chopped LINDOR Truffles, followed by the chocolate. Whisk until melted and smooth.

3. Pour into a large mug, top with a dollop of whipped cream, a drizzle of melted chocolate and a sprinkle of chocolate shavings.

CHOCOLATIER'S TIP
Get creative and try different flavours of LINDOR – our 70% Dark Chocolate is perfect for a rich and intense flavour, or why not try our Blood Orange for a zesty chocolate orange twist?

MILK CHOCOLATE AND MACADAMIA COOKIES

Take your favourite chocolate chip cookie recipe to the next level with our beautifully smooth EXCELLENCE Extra Creamy Milk Chocolate, combined with moreish macadamia nuts for that all-important crunch!

MAKES: 16–20
PREP: 25 mins
COOK: 12 mins

175g plain flour
½ tsp bicarbonate of soda
Pinch of salt
75g unsalted butter
115g light brown sugar
50g caster sugar
1 large egg
1 tsp vanilla extract
175g **Lindt EXCELLENCE Extra Creamy Milk Chocolate**, chopped (see Tip)
60g macadamia nuts, roughly chopped

1. Preheat the oven to 180°C/160°C Fan/Gas 4. Line several baking sheets with baking paper.

2. Mix together the flour, bicarbonate of soda and salt and set aside.

3. Beat together the butter and sugars in a stand mixer on medium-high speed for 3–4 minutes until pale and fluffy (scraping down the sides of the bowl as needed) – you could do this by hand in a large mixing bowl with a wooden spoon but it will take a little longer.

4. Beat in the egg followed by the vanilla extract and flour mix. Mix until you have a smooth dough.

5. Stir in the chopped chocolate and nuts until evenly distributed throughout the dough.

6. Roll the cookie dough into 50g balls and press down to flatten slightly into puck shapes. Make sure they are well spaced (about 5cm) apart. You may have to bake them in batches.

7. Bake in the oven for 10–12 minutes – turning the trays halfway through – until the edges have set and turned golden. The exact time will depend on the size of your cookies and whether you prefer them slightly gooey or a little crispy.

8. Leave to cool on the baking sheets for 10 minutes before transferring to a wire rack to finish cooling completely.

CHOCOLATIER'S TIP
You can swap our smooth EXCELLENCE Extra Creamy Milk Chocolate for our richer EXCELLENCE 70% Dark Chocolate if you prefer a more intense chocolate flavour.

EVERYDAY

DARK CHOCOLATE AND COCONUT ENERGY BALLS

These quick and easy no-bake energy balls are perfect for a healthy on-the-go snack; packed full of healthy fats, protein and fibre.

MAKES: 12
PREP: 20 mins + chilling

100g roasted almonds
5 squares **Lindt EXCELLENCE 70% Dark Chocolate** (see Tip)
1 tbsp jumbo oats
75g pitted Medjool dates
1–2 tbsp maple syrup
3 tbsp almond butter

TO DECORATE:
Desiccated coconut (see Tip)

1. Put the almonds into a food processor and blitz to crumbs. Add the chocolate and oats and blitz again until you have the consistency of breadcrumbs.

2. Add the dates, 1 tablespoon of maple syrup and the almond butter. Pulse to combine. Taste to check the sweetness and add a little more maple syrup, if wished. Tip into a bowl.

3. Line a baking sheet with greaseproof paper and sprinkle with desiccated coconut in an even layer.

4. Shape the mix into 12 balls. Roll each ball individually in the desiccated coconut.

5. Set onto a plate. Cover and chill for 20 minutes to firm up.

CHOCOLATIER'S TIP
Get creative and ring the changes by making this recipe with Lindt EXCELLENCE Caramelised Hazelnut Dark Chocolate and coating the balls with crushed hazelnuts instead of coconut.

CHOCOLATE MOUSSE CAKE WITH BERRIES

Looking for a quick and easy dessert that still has the 'wow' factor? This luxurious chocolate mousse cake is the perfect solution thanks to our exquisite EXCELLENCE 70% Dark Chocolate. You can up the indulgence further with a silky smooth chocolate topping or keep it simple and serve with fresh berries (and perhaps a scoop of ice cream!)…

SERVES: 4
PREP: 20 mins + cooling
COOK: 18 mins

FOR THE MOUSSE CAKE:
Vegetable oil, for greasing
100g **Lindt EXCELLENCE 70% Dark Chocolate**, chopped
5 medium eggs, separated

FOR THE TOPPING (OPTIONAL):
70g **Lindt EXCELLENCE 70% Dark Chocolate**, finely chopped
90ml double cream

1. For the mousse cake, preheat the oven to 160°C/140°C Fan/ Gas 3. Grease and line a small non-stick, ovenproof bowl (around 18cm diameter, 12cm deep that can hold 700ml volume) with greaseproof paper, place in a deep roasting tin and set aside.

2. Place the chopped chocolate into a heatproof bowl set over a pan of barely simmering water, ensuring the bottom of the bowl doesn't come into contact with the water, then stir until melted. Alternatively, pop the chocolate into a microwave-safe bowl and melt in 30-second bursts, stirring between each. Remove from the heat and leave to cool.

3. Once slightly cooled, stir in the egg yolks.

4. Meanwhile, in a separate bowl, whisk the egg whites until you have stiff peaks.

5. Carefully fold the egg whites into the cooled chocolate mixture with a spatula or large spoon.

6. Pour the mixture into the prepared bowl and fill the roasting tin with a kettleful of boiling water until around halfway up the sides of the bowl. Bake in the oven for about 12 minutes – or until just set on top with a slight crust, but still wobbly underneath. Remove the tin from the oven but leave the bowl to stand in the boiling water for another 5 minutes.

7. Carefully lift the bowl from the hot water and set aside to cool completely. Once cool, turn out onto a flat plate.

8. If you are making the topping, place the chopped chocolate into a heatproof bowl and set aside.

TO SERVE:

Fresh berries of
your choice – such
as raspberries,
strawberries, cherries
and blueberries
(see Tip)

9. Meanwhile, pour the cream into a small saucepan and slowly bring to a simmer.

10. Remove from the heat, pour the hot cream over the chopped chocolate and stir until melted and smooth. Leave to stand for about 5 minutes to thicken slightly.

11. Using a palette knife, spread the topping over the cooled mousse cake. Top with your choice of berries.

CHOCOLATIER'S TIP
Our Master Chocolatiers
recommend using
seasonal berries where
possible. Alternatively,
you could use frozen
berries and make your
own berry coulis.

CHOCOLATE AND AMARETTI AFFOGATO

Up the indulgence factor of a traditional affogato (vanilla ice cream 'drowning' in a shot of strong espresso) by finishing with a sprinkling of our luxurious EXCELLENCE 85% Dark Chocolate. A delicious, sophisticated dessert.

SERVES: 2
PREP: 5 mins

2–4 scoops of good-
  quality vanilla ice cream
125ml freshly brewed
  strong espresso coffee
40g amaretti biscuits,
  crumbled
50g **Lindt EXCELLENCE
  85% Dark Chocolate**,
  grated into curls

1. Set out 2 heatproof glasses or coffee cups.

2. Put 1–2 scoops of vanilla ice cream into each. Pour over the espresso, sprinkle with the crumbled amaretti and the grated chocolate curls.

3. Serve straight away.

CHOCOLATIER'S TIP
For a family-friendly version, swap the strong espresso for hot chocolate.

CHOCOLATE, PECAN AND CRANBERRY COOKIE BARS

A cross between cookies and granola bars, these fabulously fruity bars are packed full of oats, nuts and seeds – making them a good source of fibre and just the thing for an on-the-go breakfast or healthy-ish homemade snack.

MAKES: 12–15
PREP: 15 mins + cooling
** and setting**
COOK: 30 mins

125ml olive oil, plus extra
  for greasing
115g soft dark brown sugar
1 large egg
1 tsp vanilla extract
100g plain flour
4 tbsp milled flaxseeds
4 tbsp pumpkin seeds
½ tsp bicarbonate of soda
½ tsp ground cinnamon
Pinch of salt
140g jumbo oats
100g **Lindt EXCELLENCE**
  85% Dark Chocolate,
  roughly chopped
75g dried cranberries
  (see Tip)
100g pecans, roughly
  chopped

TO DECORATE
(OPTIONAL):
250g **Lindt EXCELLENCE**
  85% Dark Chocolate,
  roughly chopped

1. Preheat the oven to 180°C/160°C Fan/Gas 4. Grease and line a 28 x 18cm baking tin with greaseproof paper.

2. In the bowl of a stand mixer, beat together the olive oil and sugar for 1–2 minutes or until well combined. Add the egg and vanilla extract and beat for a further minute.

3. Add in the flour, flaxseeds, pumpkin seeds, bicarbonate of soda, cinnamon, salt and oats. Beat for 1–2 minutes, on medium speed, until the mix comes together to form a dough.

4. Fold in the chopped chocolate, dried cranberries and chopped pecans until evenly distributed throughout the dough.

5. Spoon into the prepared tin and press down evenly, using the back of your spoon, until smooth. Bake for 25–30 minutes until golden brown.

6. Leave to cool in the tin for 10 minutes before removing from the tin and transferring to a wire rack to finish cooling completely (at least 2 hours). Slice into 12–15 equal-sized bars.

7. If decorating the bars, line 2 baking trays with greaseproof paper. Melt the chocolate in a heatproof bowl over a pan of barely simmering water, ensuring the bottom of the bowl doesn't make contact with the water, then stir until melted. Alternatively, pop the chocolate into a microwave-safe bowl and melt in 30-second bursts, stirring between each.

8. One at a time, immerse the corner of a bar in the chocolate and transfer to the prepared baking trays. Place in the fridge for 10–20 minutes to set.

CHOCOLATIER'S TIP
Ring the changes by swapping the dried cranberries for raisins, chopped dried apricots or mixed dried fruit.

MILK CHOCOLATE SKILLET BROWNIE

Our luxuriously smooth and creamy Swiss GOLD Milk Chocolate Bar
makes this fabulously fudgy brownie extra indulgent – perfect for sharing
with friends and family.

SERVES: 12–14
PREP: 20 mins
COOK: 40 mins

225g unsalted butter,
   diced, plus extra for
   greasing
300g **Lindt GOLD Milk**
   Chocolate Bar, finely
   chopped (see Tip)
200g soft light brown
   sugar
100g caster sugar
4 large eggs
2 tsp vanilla extract
180g plain flour
4 tbsp cocoa powder
Pinch of salt

TO SERVE:
Scoops of good-quality
   vanilla ice cream
Lindt EXCELLENCE
   70% Dark Chocolate,
   melted, or **Lindt**
   Hazelnut Chocolate
   Spread

1. Preheat the oven to 160°C/140°C Fan/Gas 3. Grease a 30cm, ovenproof, deep cast-iron frying pan.

2. Put the chocolate into a heatproof bowl set over a pan of barely simmering water, ensuring the bottom of the bowl doesn't come into contact with the water, then stir until melted. Alternatively, pop into a microwave-safe bowl and melt in 30-second bursts, stirring between each. Remove from the heat and leave to cool.

3. Mix together the sugars and eggs with an electric mixer until light, fluffy and doubled in size (it will take 3–4 minutes on high speed).

4. Beat in the vanilla extract and cooled chocolate mix until smooth.

5. Add the flour, cocoa powder and salt and beat until just combined.

6. Tip into the prepared frying pan and bake for 30–40 minutes until the top has set but there is a slight wobble in the centre. Leave to cool for 5–10 minutes or completely if you want to serve clean slices.

7. Serve warm or cold, topped with scoops of good-quality vanilla ice cream and drizzled with melted chocolate or Hazelnut Chocolate Spread.

   TIP: If you want to easily remove the brownie from the pan, put a circle of baking paper at the bottom of your pan before cooking and just lift out.

   Photograph overleaf →

CHOCOLATIER'S TIP
If you prefer a more intense chocolate flavour, swap the GOLD Milk Chocolate Bar for our EXCELLENCE 70% Dark Chocolate.

CHOCOLATE AND ESPRESSO MILKSHAKE

Need something to set you up for the day? Take your morning coffee to new heights with our adult-only milkshake, combining our intense EXCELLENCE 70% Dark Chocolate with a jolt of espresso and a hint of sweet cinnamon (and it's vegan-friendly, too). The perfect way to start your day in style.

SERVES: 2
PREP: 5 mins

710ml unsweetened almond milk (see Tip)
1 large ripe banana, sliced
4 dates, pitted and roughly chopped
½ tsp ground cinnamon
2 shots of espresso, cooled
40g **Lindt EXCELLENCE 70% Dark Chocolate**, finely chopped (see Tip)

TO SERVE:
Lindt EXCELLENCE 70% Dark Chocolate (see Tip), melted
Chocolate shavings

1. Pour the almond milk into a blender. Add the banana, dates, cinnamon and espresso. Blend on high speed for about 30 seconds or until smooth.

2. Add the finely chopped chocolate and blend for a further minute or until you have your desired consistency (you may enjoy a few fine chunks of chocolate).

3. Pour into 2 tall glasses, drizzle with melted chocolate and sprinkle with chocolate shavings. Enjoy!

CHOCOLATIER'S TIP
You can also use hazelnut milk if you prefer. Our EXCELLENCE 85%, 90% and 99% Dark Chocolate Bars are also vegan-friendly, so you can increase the cocoa percentage and enjoy a more intense chocolate flavour.

DARK CHOCOLATE AND HAZELNUT MUG BROWNIE

Microwaving in a mug is ideal for when you want a comforting pudding in minutes. Mug cakes have been around for a while, so our Lindt Master Chocolatiers thought they would go one step further and they created this fudgy dark chocolate and roasted hazelnut brownie recipe, which is ultra-indulgent and utterly irresistible...

SERVES: 1
PREP: 5 mins
COOK: 70 seconds

40g self-raising flour
10g cocoa powder
25g soft brown sugar
4–5 tbsp full-fat milk
30g butter, melted
35g **Lindt EXCELLENCE Caramelised Hazelnut Dark Chocolate,** finely chopped (see Tip)

1. In a medium bowl, whisk together the flour, cocoa powder and sugar.

2. Whisk in the milk, followed by the melted butter until you have a smooth batter.

3. Spoon half the batter into a large microwave-safe mug that holds around 350ml, sprinkle in two-thirds of the finely chopped Lindt EXCELLENCE Roasted Hazelnut Dark Chocolate, before topping with the remaining batter. Nestle in the remaining finely chopped chocolate.

4. Set onto a microwave-safe plate and microwave for about 70 seconds – it may take a little longer (up to 90 seconds), the exact time will vary depending on your microwave and the dimensions of your mug.

5. Carefully remove from the microwave (it will be hot!) and leave to stand for 10 seconds.

6. Grab a spoon and enjoy!

CHOCOLATIER'S TIP
Why not try our EXCELLENCE Dark Cranberry, Almond and Hazelnut Chocolate for a delicious fruit and nut combination? Alternatively, use 15g finely chopped EXCELLENCE White Chocolate with a Touch of Vanilla and 15g finely chopped EXCELLENCE Extra Creamy Milk Chocolate for a decadent double chocolate option.

MATCHA AND WHITE CHOCOLATE MUFFINS

A matcha made in heaven… the slight bitterness of matcha marries with the sweetness of our Lindt EXCELLENCE White Chocolate with a Touch of Vanilla to create these moreish muffins. A delicious grab-and-go breakfast or brilliant bake for a grown-up gathering; from coffee mornings to office birthdays.

MAKES: 8–10
PREP: 15 mins
COOK: 25 mins

200g self-raising flour
125g caster sugar
Pinch of salt
1½ tbsp matcha powder, plus extra for dusting
1 large egg
65ml vegetable oil
125ml whole milk
75g **Lindt EXCELLENCE White Chocolate with a Touch of Vanilla**, roughly chopped, plus 50g melted, for drizzling

1. Preheat the oven to 170°C/150°C Fan/Gas 3. Line a muffin tin with 8 larger muffin cases or 10 small paper cases and set aside.

2. Whisk the flour, sugar, salt and matcha powder together in a large bowl.

3. Add in the egg, oil and milk and mix until you have a smooth batter.

4. Fold in 50g of the chopped chocolate — taking care not to overmix — ensuring the chocolate is evenly distributed throughout.

5. Fill the muffin cases so they're three-quarters full and sprinkle the remaining 25g of chopped chocolate on top. Bake for 20–25 minutes until a skewer inserted into the middle of the muffins comes out clean.

6. Leave to cool in the tin for 10 minutes before transferring to a wire rack to finish cooling completely. Finish with a drizzle of melted white chocolate and a sprinkling of matcha powder.

CHOCOLATIER'S TIP
If you like intense flavour combinations, swap our EXCELLENCE White Chocolate with a Touch of Vanilla for our decadent EXCELLENCE 70% Dark Chocolate.

CHOCOLATE LINZER BISCUITS

Our Lindt Master Chocolatiers have weaved their magic on the
classic Austrian Linzer biscuit – famous for its delicious fruity jam
filling – by adding our decadent EXCELLENCE 85% Dark Chocolate.
A truly irresistible treat.

MAKES: 30–36 biscuits
PREP: 45 mins + chilling
COOK: 12 mins

100g **Lindt EXCELLENCE
   85% Dark Chocolate**,
   finely chopped
270g plain flour
50g ground almonds
4 tbsp cocoa powder,
   plus extra for dusting
Pinch of salt
225g unsalted butter,
   at room temperature
115g caster sugar
115g soft light brown sugar
1 large egg
1 tsp vanilla extract
165g raspberry jam
   (see Tip overleaf)

1. Put the chopped chocolate into a heatproof bowl set over a
   pan of barely simmering water, ensuring the bottom of the bowl
   doesn't come into contact with the water, then stir until melted.
   Alternatively, pop the chocolate into a microwave-safe bowl and
   melt in 30-second bursts, stirring between each. Remove from the
   heat and leave to cool.

2. In a separate bowl, whisk together the flour, ground almonds, cocoa
   powder and salt.

3. In the bowl of a stand mixer (or use a large bowl with an electric
   hand mixer), beat together the butter and sugars on medium-high
   speed for about 1 minute or until well combined, scraping down the
   sides as necessary.

4. Beat in the egg and vanilla extract, followed by the melted chocolate,
   until well combined. Tip in the flour mix and mix on a low speed until
   you have a smooth dough.

5. Divide in half, flatten to puck-shaped discs, wrap in cling film or
   greaseproof paper and chill for 1 hour in the fridge.

6. Line a couple of large baking trays with baking paper.

7. To roll: dust another large sheet of baking paper with cocoa powder
   and place 1 disc on top. Lightly dust the dough with cocoa and top
   with another sheet of baking paper. Roll out the dough to about
   3mm thick (no thicker than 6mm). Use a 5cm fluted round cutter
   to cut out rounds. Repeat with the remaining disc of dough, making
   sure you have an even number.

Method continued overleaf →

CHOCOLATE LINZER BISCUITS *continued*

8. Using a 2cm or 2.5cm round or star cutter, cut out the centre of half of the rounds. Re-roll the scraps. Place the biscuits 2.5cm apart on the prepared baking trays. Chill for 30 minutes.

9. Preheat the oven to 180°C/160°C Fan/Gas 4.

10. Bake the biscuits for 10–12 minutes or until the edges are firm – you may have to do this in batches. Leave to cool on the baking trays for 5 minutes before transferring to a wire rack to finish cooling completely.

11. Spread around 1 tsp jam on the bottom of each of the whole biscuits and sandwich with the cut-out biscuits on top.

CHOCOLATIER'S TIP
We used raspberry jam in this recipe but you can experiment with different flavours of jam and fruit spread – strawberry and cherry flavours also work well.

CHOCOLATE AND PEANUT BUTTER POPCORN

Popcorn is the ultimate movie night treat! We have put our own luxury
Lindt twist on this snacking staple with a peanut butter and EXCELLENCE
Sea Salt Dark Chocolate combo. Perfect for parties or divided into
portions to enjoy as an indulgent on-the-go snack.

SERVES: 8–10
 (makes 12 cups)
PREP: 10 mins + cooling
 and setting
COOK: 45 mins

90g corn kernels
3 tbsp vegetable oil
65g peanuts, roughly
 chopped
115g unsalted butter
200g dark brown sugar
70ml golden syrup
70g smooth peanut butter
½ tsp bicarbonate of soda
1 tsp vanilla extract
1 tsp salt
100g **Lindt EXCELLENCE**
 Sea Salt Dark
 Chocolate, chopped
 (see Tip)

1. Preheat the oven to 140°C/120°C Fan/Gas 1 and line a baking tray with greaseproof paper. Set aside.

2. Begin by popping the corn: tip the corn kernels into a medium saucepan that has a tight-fitting lid and pour in the vegetable oil. Stir to coat the kernels in the oil. Pop the lid on and place over a medium heat until you hear the first pop, then turn the heat to medium-low. When you begin to hear lots of popping, give the pan a shake (using oven gloves as the pan will be hot). Continue to shake frequently until the popping sound subsides. Turn off the heat and leave the lid on the pan for 5 minutes. Tip into a large heatproof mixing bowl and stir in the peanuts. Set aside.

3. Wipe out the pot you used to pop the corn and add the butter, brown sugar, golden syrup and peanut butter. Stir well.

4. Place over a medium heat and bring to the boil, stirring often. Reduce the heat slightly and continue gently bubbling, stirring often to prevent burning.

5. After 7 minutes, remove from the heat and carefully add the bicarbonate of soda, vanilla extract and salt (take care as the caramel will bubble up). Quickly, and carefully, pour over the peanut popcorn mix and stir to coat in the caramel. Tip onto the prepared baking sheet and spread into a smooth and even layer.

Method continued overleaf →

CHOCOLATE AND PEANUT BUTTER
POPCORN *continued*

6. Bake in the oven for 30 minutes – stirring every 15 minutes to turn and separate the corn. Remove from the oven and leave to cool.

7. Meanwhile, pop the chopped chocolate into a heatproof bowl set over a pan of barely simmering water, ensuring the bottom of the bowl doesn't come into contact with the water, then stir until melted. Alternatively, pop the chocolate into a microwave-safe bowl and melt in 30-second bursts, stirring between each. Remove from the heat and leave to cool.

8. Once the popcorn is cool and set, pour over the melted chocolate and gently stir to coat. Leave to set for about 1 hour before tipping into bowls and serving.

CHOCOLATIER'S TIP
We have a selection of exquisite EXCELLENCE Chocolate Bars which work beautifully for coating this buttery popcorn – get creative with your favourite flavours.

CELEBRATION

DARK CHOCOLATE BUNDT CAKE

Bundt cakes are an American take on the European Gugelhupf. Famed for their fluted shapes, these beautiful bakes will be the talk of any teatime table. We have added extra decadence with our intense EXCELLENCE 85% Dark Chocolate in the batter and a gloriously glossy ganache using our creamy vanilla-infused EXCELLENCE White Chocolate with a Touch of Vanilla.

SERVES: 8–10
PREP: 25 mins
COOK: 50 mins

225g plain flour
65g cocoa powder
2 tsp baking powder
½ tsp salt
¼ tsp bicarbonate of soda
350g caster sugar
125ml vegetable oil
2 large eggs
1 tsp vanilla extract
100g **Lindt EXCELLENCE 85% Dark Chocolate**, melted and cooled
300ml full-fat milk

FOR THE GANACHE:
Butter, for greasing
100g **Lindt EXCELLENCE White Chocolate with a Touch of Vanilla**, finely chopped
3 tbsp double cream

1. Preheat the oven to 180°C/160°C Fan/Gas 4. Generously butter a 2.4–2.8 L Bundt tin.

2. In a medium bowl, sift the flour with the cocoa powder, baking powder, salt and bicarbonate of soda. Set aside.

3. In the bowl of a stand mixer fitted with the paddle attachment, beat the sugar with the oil, eggs and vanilla extract on low speed until just combined. Slowly stream in the melted chocolate until incorporated. You could also do this in a bowl with a wooden spoon, but it will take a little longer.

4. Beat in half of the flour mixture, then half of the milk. Repeat alternate additions until you have a smooth batter.

5. Spoon the batter into the prepared tin and smooth over the top. Bake in the centre of the oven for 45–50 minutes or until a skewer inserted into the centre of the cake comes out clean. Leave to cool in the tin for 10 minutes with a plate over the top (the steam produced will help release it from the tin) before turning out onto a wire rack to finish cooling completely.

6. For the ganache: pop the finely chopped EXCELLENCE White Chocolate with a Touch of Vanilla and double cream into a microwave-safe bowl. Microwave for 20 seconds and stir. Continue to microwave in 5-second increments, stirring in between, until melted and smooth. Once completely melted, leave to stand for 5 minutes.

7. Set the cooled bundt cake onto a flat plate and spoon over the white chocolate and vanilla ganache.

CHOCOLATIER'S TIP
Make sure you butter the tin thoroughly to ensure the baked cake comes out cleanly.

CARAMEL AND CHOCOLATE FONDANT CAKE

A smooth, creamy and indulgent cake with a gooey fondant centre.
Pure chocolate heaven for true chocolate lovers.

SERVES: 10–12
PREP: 20 mins + chilling
COOK: 1 hour 5 mins

200g **Lindt EXCELLENCE
  70% Dark Chocolate,**
  or **Lindt COOKING
  70% Dark Intense**,
  chopped
200g salted butter, diced,
  plus extra for greasing
4 large eggs
200g caster sugar
100g caramel, plus extra
  to serve
35g cornflour
2 tbsp cocoa powder,
  for dusting

1. Preheat the oven to 210°C/190°C Fan/Gas 7. Grease and line the base and sides of a deep 20cm round cake tin.

2. Put the chopped chocolate and butter into a heatproof bowl set over a pan of barely simmering water, ensuring the bottom of the bowl doesn't come into contact with the water. Melt the butter and chocolate, stirring often (alternatively, pop both into a microwave-safe bowl and melt in 30-second bursts, stirring between each until smooth). Remove from the heat and set aside.

3. In a separate bowl, whisk the eggs with the sugar until light and pale.

4. Stir the caramel into the melted chocolate mix and gently fold into the whisked eggs.

5. Fold in the cornflour.

6. Bake for 5 minutes, then reduce the temperature to 160°C/140°C Fan/Gas 3 and bake for 50–60 minutes or until the centre is just firm to the touch (it should be soft but not runny). Leave to cool completely – don't worry if it cracks and sinks slightly. Cover with cling film and chill in the fridge for at least 4 hours, or ideally overnight.

7. Remove the cake from the tin and set it onto a flat plate. Cut slices using a hot, clean knife (run it under boiling water and wipe dry before slicing). Serve at room temperature with a dusting of cocoa powder and a drizzle of caramel on the side.

CHOCOLATIER'S TIP
Serve with a scoop of melting vanilla ice cream or a handful of fruity berries for a final flourish.

LUXURY MOCHA CAKE

Our Lindt Master Chocolatiers have created the most decadent mocha cake with a chocolate and cream cheese filling and topped with a rich chocolate glaze.

SERVES: 12
PREP: 1 hour + chilling
COOK: 30 mins

FOR THE CAKE:
200g unsalted butter,
  at room temperature,
  plus extra for greasing
325g plain flour, plus
  extra for dusting
100g **Lindt EXCELLENCE
  70% Dark Chocolate**,
  finely chopped
60g cocoa powder, sifted
250ml freshly brewed
  hot coffee
Pinch of salt
1 tsp baking powder
1 tsp bicarbonate of soda
235g caster sugar
140g brown sugar
3 eggs
2 tsp vanilla extract
175ml buttermilk

1. For the cake, preheat the oven to 180°C/160°C Fan/Gas 4. Grease and flour three 20cm round cake tins and line the bottoms with baking paper. Set aside.

2. Combine the chopped chocolate and cocoa powder in a heatproof bowl. Pour the hot coffee over the top. Leave to sit for 2 minutes, then whisk until smooth and leave to cool to room temperature.

3. In a large bowl, whisk together the flour, salt, baking powder and bicarbonate of soda. Set aside.

4. In the bowl of a stand mixer, beat together the butter and sugars until light and fluffy. Add the eggs one at a time, beating between each addition until incorporated. Beat in the vanilla extract, followed by the cooled chocolate mixture.

5. With the mixer on low, alternately add the dry mixture in 3 parts with the buttermilk in 2 parts, starting and ending with the dry. Scrape the bowl as needed between additions.

6. Divide the cake batter equally between the prepared tins and smooth the top. Bake for 25–30 minutes or until a skewer inserted into the centre of the cake comes out clean. Cool completely in the tins on a wire rack. Once cold, remove from the tins.

7. For the frosting, beat the cream cheese with an electric whisk until light and fluffy. Beat in the butter until blended and smooth. Beat in the melted and cooled chocolate and the cocoa powder, followed by the icing sugar until blended. Beat in the sour cream and vanilla extract until creamy. If the frosting is too soft to spread, chill for 15–20 minutes to firm up.

FOR THE FUDGY CREAM
  CHEESE CHOCOLATE
  FROSTING:
250g full-fat cream
  cheese, at room
  temperature
45g unsalted butter,
  at room temperature
100g **Lindt EXCELLENCE**
  70% Dark Chocolate,
  melted and cooled
30g cocoa powder, sifted
265g icing sugar, sifted
80g sour cream
1 tsp vanilla extract

FOR THE GLAZE:
200ml single cream
200g **Lindt EXCELLENCE**
  70% Dark Chocolate,
  finely chopped
75g unsalted butter,
  cut into cubes, at
  room temperature

TO DECORATE:
1 **Lindt TEDDY**,
  unwrapped (see Tip)

8. Place one cake on a flat plate or cake board; spread the top with half of the frosting. Top with another cake and spread the remaining frosting on top. Top with the remaining cake. Cover and chill for 2–3 hours to set the frosting before glazing.

9. For the glaze, pour the cream into a small saucepan over a medium heat, stirring until just steaming. Remove from the heat and stir in the chopped chocolate and butter until melted and smooth.

10. Place the cake on a wire rack above a plate or tray large enough to catch the excess glaze. Pour the glaze over the top and smooth over with a spatula. Chill for 1–2 hours until the glaze has set.

11. Transfer the cake to a flat serving plate. Decorate with the Lindt TEDDY.

CHOCOLATIER'S TIP

For a smooth chocolate glaze, top the cake as soon as the butter has been incorporated. If you prefer to see traces of the spatula on the finished glaze, wait a few minutes before spreading to allow the glaze to harden slightly.

Our TEDDY is the perfect centrepiece for Christmas, but you can also make this throughout the year and decorate with our LINDOR Truffles, juicy FRUIT SENSATIONS or irresistible CRISPY SENSATIONS – not forgetting our luxurious Lindt SWISS LUXURY SELECTION Pralines.

DOUBLE CHOCOLATE CHEESECAKE

Discover chocolate decadence with these luxurious cheesecake slices
– topped off with a drizzle of our EXCELLENCE 70% Dark Chocolate.

SERVES: 12
PREP: 35 mins + chilling

FOR THE BASE:
325g bourbon biscuits
100g unsalted butter,
  melted
Pinch of salt

FOR THE CHEESECAKE:
2 tbsp cocoa powder
350g full-fat cream
  cheese, at room
  temperature
200g caster sugar
250g **Lindt EXCELLENCE
  80% Dark Chocolate**,
  melted and cooled
300ml double cream

TO DECORATE:
50g **Lindt EXCELLENCE
  80% Dark Chocolate**,
  melted and cooled

1. Line a loose-bottomed 20 x 30cm tin. Either blitz the bourbon biscuits in a food processor until they are fine crumbs or bash them with a rolling pin. Mix the biscuit crumbs with the melted butter and salt, and tip them into the prepared tin. Press down either with your hands or the back of a spoon so that there's a compacted, level layer of biscuit crumbs. Put in the fridge to set for 15 minutes.

2. Mix together the cocoa powder, cream cheese and caster sugar until smooth and fluffy, then gradually pour in the melted chocolate while beating with an electric whisk until combined.

3. Add in the cream and beat again with an electric whisk until combined. Spoon on top of the biscuit base and smooth into an even layer with the back of a spoon.

4. To decorate, drizzle over the extra dark chocolate in swirls. Place in the fridge and leave to set for 4–5 hours.

5. Slice into rectangles with a hot knife before serving.

CHOCOLATIER'S TIP
For a hint of floral flavour, add 2 tsp rose water to the cheesecake mixture.

CHOCOLATE VANILLA CUSTARD SLICES

Our Lindt Master Chocolatiers have weaved their magic into the classic custard slice. Prepare to indulge in a rich chocolate and vanilla custard sandwiched between layers of irresistibly buttery puff pastry. This is the perfect afternoon tea treat.

MAKES: 15–20
PREP: 15 mins + cooling and chilling
COOK: 20 mins

2 x 320g sheets good-quality all-butter puff pastry
30g custard powder
3 large egg yolks
50g caster sugar
250ml whole milk
190ml double cream
40g unsalted butter
2 tsp vanilla extract
160g **Lindt EXCELLENCE 70% Dark Chocolate**, chopped

TO SERVE:
Icing sugar, for dusting

1. Preheat the oven to 200°C/180°C Fan/Gas 6.

2. Line 2 baking trays with baking paper. Unroll the pastry sheets and set one onto each of the prepared trays. Using a fork, prick holes all over the surface. Top with another sheet of baking paper and weigh down with another baking tray (this will prevent them puffing up too much). Bake for 16–18 minutes or until golden. Set aside to cool completely.

3. Meanwhile, make the custard. Mix together the custard powder, egg yolks and sugar with 1 tablespoon of the milk in a heatproof bowl to form a smooth paste. Set aside.

4. Pour the remaining milk and the cream into a saucepan. Add the butter and vanilla extract and slowly bring to the boil, stirring often.

5. Pour a little of the hot cream mixture onto the egg yolk mixture and mix well to combine. Pour this blend into the hot cream in the pan and return to the hob. Cook over a low heat, stirring all the time, for about 1 minute – or until thickened.

6. Remove from the heat and stir in the chopped chocolate until melted and smooth. Pour into a heatproof bowl, cover with cling film and leave to cool completely.

7. To assemble, place one sheet of the cooked pastry onto a flat board. Spoon over the custard and, using a palette knife, spread in a smooth, thick layer. Top with the second sheet of pastry and gently press down. Chill for 2–3 hours or until firmly set. Dust with icing sugar and cut into 12–15 slices with a sharp knife..

CHOCOLATIER'S TIP
You can also add a layer of fresh raspberries before topping with the second sheet of puff pastry for a fruity flavour.

DOUBLE CHOCOLATE RASPBERRY BROWNIE SUNDAE

This divine dessert is perfect for a dinner party treat using our fabulously fruity and deliciously decadent EXCELLENCE Raspberry Intense Dark Chocolate combined with our sweet and creamy EXCELLENCE White Chocolate with a Touch of Vanilla...

SERVES: 6
PREP: 25 mins + chilling

FOR THE SHARDS:
100g **Lindt EXCELLENCE White Chocolate with a Touch of Vanilla**, chopped
A couple of drops of pink food colouring gel

FOR THE SUNDAE:
100g **Lindt EXCELLENCE Raspberry Intense Dark Chocolate**, chopped
6 brownies
12 scoops of good-quality vanilla ice cream
250g fresh raspberries

TO DECORATE (OPTIONAL):
Freeze-dried raspberries
Sprinkles

CHOCOLATIER'S TIP
If you are in a hurry, simply top with a square of EXCELLENCE White Chocolate with a Touch of Vanilla.

1. For the shards: place the chopped white chocolate in a heatproof bowl set over a pan of barely simmering water, ensuring the bottom of the bowl doesn't come into contact with the water, then stir until melted. Alternatively, pop the chocolate into a microwave-safe bowl and melt in 30-second bursts, stirring between each.

2. Line a baking sheet with greaseproof paper. Using a palette knife, spread the melted chocolate onto the centre of the sheet, in a strip about 38cm long, leaving a 2.5cm border around the edge.

3. Dot with pink food colouring gel randomly and swirl together with a cocktail stick to create a marbled effect. Chill in the fridge for 2–3 hours or until the chocolate hardens and has set.

4. Crack the chocolate with a rolling pin to create shards. Slide the marbled shards onto a baking sheet lined with baking paper, then chill until ready to use.

5. For the sundae: place the EXCELLENCE Raspberry Intense Dark Chocolate in a heatproof bowl set over a saucepan of barely simmering water as in step 1, stirring until the chocolate is melted and smooth – there will be flecks of raspberries. Remove from the heat and pour into a jug.

6. Set out 6 tall glasses or sundae dishes. Crumble half a brownie into the bottom of each glass. Sprinkle with a couple of fresh raspberries and top with 2 scoops of vanilla ice cream. Repeat with another brownie half and more raspberries.

7. Drizzle with the melted EXCELLENCE Raspberry Intense Dark Chocolate and top with a marbled white chocolate shard. Finish with freeze-dried raspberries and sprinkles, if you like. Serve straight away.

Photograph overleaf →

MINI MOCHA ECLAIRS

Our luxurious Lindt chocolate makes the classic French eclair even more irresistible. This recipe, featuring an intense EXCELLENCE 70% Dark Chocolate glaze and EXCELLENCE Extra Creamy Milk Chocolate and espresso cream filling, is sure to become an afternoon tea favourite.

MAKES: 16–20
PREP: 30 mins + chilling
COOK: 35 mins

FOR THE MOCHA CREAM:
450ml double cream
75g caster sugar
1½ tbsp instant espresso
   powder
225g **Lindt EXCELLENCE
   Extra Creamy Milk
   Chocolate**, finely
   chopped

FOR THE CHOUX PASTRY:
80ml water
80ml whole milk
75g unsalted butter
80g plain flour
Generous pinch of salt
2 eggs, beaten

FOR THE CHOCOLATE
   GLAZE:
100g **Lindt EXCELLENCE
   70% Dark Chocolate**,
   melted

1. For the mocha cream, pour the cream into a saucepan. Add the sugar and espresso powder and slowly bring to a simmer, stirring often. Add the chopped chocolate and stir until you have a smooth, melted chocolate, coffee-infused cream. Remove from the heat and pour into a heatproof bowl. Leave to cool completely before covering and chilling in the fridge for 2 hours until set.

2. Meanwhile, for the choux pastry, preheat the oven to 200°C/180°C Fan/Gas 6. Line a couple of flat baking trays with baking paper.

3. Pour the water and milk into a medium-sized saucepan. Add the butter and heat gently until melted, stirring often. Increase the heat until the liquid comes to the boil. Tip in the flour and salt and beat vigorously with a wooden spoon until you have a smooth dough that just comes away from the sides of the pan. Spoon into a bowl and leave to cool for a few minutes.

4. Once cool, gradually add the eggs, beating until a smooth dough is formed that just falls off the spoon – you may not need all the beaten egg mixture.

5. Transfer into a piping bag with a medium-sized plain nozzle. Then pipe approximately 16–20 eclairs (about 6–7cm long) well-spaced apart onto the prepared baking sheets. Bake for 18–20 minutes until golden.

CHOCOLATIER'S TIP
If you cannot find our EXCELLENCE Extra Creamy Milk Chocolate, take the time to explore our range of smooth milk chocolates – they all bring their unique chocolate flavour profiles to this delicious recipe.

6. Using a cocktail stick, make a small hole in the bottom of each eclair, turn upside down and return to the oven for 5 minutes. Remove from the oven and leave to cool on the baking sheets for 5 minutes before transferring to wire racks to finish cooling completely.

7. Dip the cooled eclairs into the melted chocolate and leave to set.

8. Meanwhile, remove the mocha cream from the fridge and, using an electric whisk, whisk until stiff enough to pipe. Spoon into a piping bag fitted with a star nozzle.

9. Once the chocolate glaze has set, gently halve the eclairs lengthways with a small, serrated knife. Pipe swirls of the mocha cream on the bottom half before gently sandwiching with the glazed half. Repeat with the remaining eclairs.

10. Enjoy with a cup of tea or coffee – or as a delicious dessert.

FIG AND HAZELNUT CHOCOLATE TORTE

Looking for a delicious cake with extra 'wow' factor? Try this impressive triple-tiered hazelnut torte with a heavenly hazelnut buttercream and juicy fig decoration. The perfect way to celebrate any special occasion.

SERVES: 8–10
PREP: 40 mins + cooling
COOK: 25 mins

FOR THE HAZELNUT
  SPONGE CAKE:
Butter, for greasing
180g plain flour
2 tsp baking powder
¼ tsp salt
7 medium eggs, separated
235g caster sugar
100ml water
60g ground hazelnuts
1 tsp vanilla extract

FOR THE CHOCOLATE
  HAZELNUT ICING:
225g unsalted butter, at
  room temperature
200g **Lindt EXCELLENCE
  70% Dark Chocolate**,
  melted and cooled
100g **Lindt Hazelnut
  Chocolate Spread**
60g cocoa powder, sifted
375g icing sugar, sifted
125ml double cream

Ingredients continued
overleaf →

1. For the hazelnut sponge cake: preheat the oven to 180°C/160°C Fan/Gas 4. Grease and line the bottom of three 20cm round cake tins and set aside.

2. In a large bowl, sift together the flour, baking powder and salt; set aside.

3. Beat together the egg yolks and sugar in a mixing bowl until thick and lemony-coloured. Slowly beat in the water until incorporated. Sift the flour mixture over the top and stir until blended. Fold in the ground hazelnuts and vanilla extract.

4. In a separate clean bowl, beat the egg whites until stiff peaks form. Fold one-third of the whisked egg whites into the yolk mixture. Fold in the remaining whites one-third at a time until combined. Divide equally between the prepared tins and smooth over the tops.

5. Bake for 20–25 minutes or until a skewer comes out clean when inserted into centre of the cake and the cake springs back when lightly touched. Leave to cool in the tins for 15 minutes. Remove from the tins and leave to cool completely on wire racks.

6. Once cool, make the icing by beating the butter and cooled chocolate together until you have a smooth mixture. Add in the Hazelnut Chocolate spread, cocoa powder and icing sugar and beat until combined, then pour in the double cream and beat until you have a smooth, soft buttercream. Put it into a piping bag with a large round nozzle.

Method continued overleaf →

FIG AND HAZELNUT CHOCOLATE TORTE *continued*

TO DECORATE:
150g hazelnuts, roasted
  and roughly chopped
**50g Lindt Hazelnut
  Chocolate Spread**
4 figs, halved or
  quartered

7. Lay one sponge down, pipe buttercream dots on top in a circle around the edge, then fill in the middle with buttercream. Sprinkle 2 tablespoons of chopped hazelnuts on top then place another sponge on top. Repeat the icing and hazelnuts and place the final sponge on top. Pipe more buttercream dots all over the surface, then fill in the gaps by piping in dots of the Hazelnut Chocolate Spread.

8. Finish by topping with the figs and remaining hazelnuts.

CHOCOLATIER'S TIP
Keep the buttercream at room temperature if using it on the same day. If not, transfer to an airtight container and refrigerate for up to 3 days – or freeze for up to 1 month. Before using, bring to room temperature and beat with the paddle attachment of a stand mixer for 4–6 minutes, on low speed, until smooth again.

CHOCOLATE CARAMEL CUPCAKES

Discover our rich and moist gluten-free chocolate cupcakes – made with
our luxurious Lindt EXCELLENCE Dark Caramel & Sea Salt Chocolate –
topped with whipped cream and a drizzle of salted caramel.

MAKES: 12
PREP: 40 mins + cooling
COOK: 30 mins

FOR THE CUPCAKES:
70g unsalted butter, at
    room temperature, plus
    extra for greasing
50g almond flour, plus
    extra for dusting
25g cocoa powder
20g cornflour
¼ tsp baking powder
95g caster sugar
4 medium eggs, separated
1 tsp vanilla extract
100g **Lindt EXCELLENCE
    Dark Caramel & Sea
    Salt Chocolate**, melted

Ingredients continued
overleaf →

1. For the cupcakes: preheat the oven to 180°C/160°C Fan/Gas 4. Grease and flour 12 muffin cups and line the bottoms with a round of greaseproof paper; set aside.

2. Whisk together the almond flour, cocoa powder, cornflour and baking powder; set aside.

3. Beat the butter and half of the sugar until light and fluffy. Gradually add the egg yolks, one at a time, making sure each is incorporated before adding the next. Beat in the vanilla extract before folding in the melted chocolate. Stir in the almond flour mix until combined.

4. In a separate clean bowl, whisk the egg whites with an electric hand mixer on medium speed until foamy. Gradually add the remaining sugar and whisk on high speed until stiff peaks start to form. Fold one-third of the egg whites into the chocolate batter before folding in the remaining egg whites until just combined.

5. Divide the batter between the prepared muffin cups so they're half to three-quarters full. Bake for 25–30 minutes or until only a few moist crumbs stick to a skewer when inserted into the centre of the cupcakes. Transfer to a wire rack and leave to cool completely.

6. Meanwhile, make the salted caramel sauce. Add the golden syrup and sugar to a medium heavy-bottomed saucepan and gently heat. Without stirring, cook for 4–6 minutes or until golden brown, gently swirling the pan to ensure the sugar is browning evenly.

Method continued overleaf →

CHOCOLATE CARAMEL CUPCAKES *continued*

FOR THE SALTED
CARAMEL SAUCE:
1 tbsp golden syrup
215g caster sugar
120ml double cream,
at room temperature
60g unsalted butter,
at room temperature
1 tsp vanilla extract
¼ tsp sea salt

FOR THE CARAMEL-
INFUSED CREAM:
250ml double cream
25g icing sugar, sifted
3 tbsp cooled salted
caramel sauce
100g **Lindt EXCELLENCE
Dark Caramel & Sea
Salt Chocolate**, cut into
diamonds along the
squares

7. Carefully add the cream, stirring slowly until combined. Cook for
2 more minutes. Remove from the heat. Stir in the butter, vanilla
extract and sea salt. Leave to cool completely (this can be stored
in airtight container in the refrigerator for up to 2 weeks).

8. For the salted caramel-infused cream: whip the cream until stiff
peaks start to form. Beat in the icing sugar, followed by half of the
cooled sauce until just combined. Spoon into a piping bag fitted
with a large round nozzle.

9. Pipe a generous amount of caramel-infused cream onto each
cupcake. Drizzle with some of the remaining salted caramel sauce.
Decorate with a diamond of Lindt EXCELLENCE Dark Caramel &
Sea Salt Chocolate. Serve straight away.

CHOCOLATIER'S TIP
If you prefer, decorate with our LINDOR Salted Caramel Truffles.
If making this recipe for someone following a gluten-free diet, always
check the manufacturer's label to ensure all your ingredients are free
from gluten.

CHOCOLATE AND CHERRY ETON MESS

Our Master Chocolatiers have put a luxury Lindt twist on this classic English dessert… imagine layers of heavenly Hazelnut Chocolate Spread, vanilla-infused cream, juicy cherries and crunchy meringue, all finished off with a sprinkling of our exquisite EXCELLENCE chocolate.

SERVES: 3–4 (the exact number will depend on the size, and shape, of your glasses)
PREP: 20 mins + cooling
COOK: 15 mins

FOR THE CREAM:
500ml double cream
1 tsp vanilla extract
150g **Lindt Hazelnut Chocolate Spread**

FOR THE CHERRIES:
400g frozen sweet cherries
About 2 tbsp brown sugar or coconut sugar, or to taste

TO ASSEMBLE:
4-5 tbsp **Lindt Hazelnut Chocolate Spread**
2 large individual meringue nests, crushed (see Tip)
2 squares **Lindt EXCELLENCE 70% Dark Chocolate**, finely grated

1. In a mixing bowl, whisk the double cream and vanilla extract to soft peaks – take care not to over-whisk. Spoon half of the cream into a separate bowl and set aside.

2. Add the Lindt Hazelnut Chocolate Spread to the remaining cream and whisk until combined and forming stiff peaks. Set aside. Cover both bowls and chill while you prepare the rest of the dessert.

3. Tip the cherries into a medium saucepan and add the sugar, to taste. Set over a low heat and bring to the boil. Reduce the heat and simmer for 5 minutes, stirring occasionally.

4. Strain the liquid into a jug, reserving the cherries in a sieve. Tip the cherries into a bowl and set aside to cool completely. Meanwhile, pour the liquid back into the pan and bring back to the boil. Boil for 5 minutes, or until slightly reduced. Remove from the heat, pour back into the jug and leave to cool completely.

5. To assemble: set out 3–4 dessert glasses. Place a generous amount of chocolate-hazelnut cream into the base of one of the glasses. Top with a generous layer of vanilla cream. Spoon over some of the cooled cherries before drizzling with the reduced cherry juice. Drizzle with a spoonful of Lindt Hazelnut Chocolate Spread. Sprinkle with crushed meringue pieces.

6. Add another layer of chocolate-hazelnut cream, followed by the vanilla cream, cherries and juice. Sprinkle with grated chocolate and crushed meringue pieces, and drizzle with extra Lindt Hazelnut Chocolate Spread. Repeat with the remaining glasses, and serve.

CHOCOLATIER'S TIP
You can use shop-bought meringue nests, but we recommend using homemade for a perfectly crisp meringue with a soft and chewy centre.

FAMILY

CHOCOLATE AND HAZELNUT FREEZER FUDGE

Try this super simple seven-ingredient fudge recipe that takes just
minutes to make. Perfect for a prep-ahead sweet treat…
Thank you to @healthyfamilyfoodideas for this recipe.

MAKES: 16–20 squares
PREP: 15 mins + freezing

Butter, for greasing
60g **Lindt EXCELLENCE
  70% Dark Chocolate**,
  chopped
110ml double cream
60g full-fat cream cheese,
  at room temperature
  (see Tip)
1 tsp vanilla paste or extract
2 tbsp hazelnut butter
1½ tbsp runny honey or
  maple syrup
Pinch of salt

TO DECORATE:
3–4 squares **Lindt
  EXCELLENCE 70%
  Dark Chocolate**,
  melted and cooled
  (see Tip)
2 tbsp roasted hazelnuts,
  chopped

1. Grease and line an 18 x 12cm tin with baking paper and set aside.

2. Place the chopped chocolate and cream into a medium-sized microwave-safe bowl and microwave for 30–40 seconds. Leave for a few minutes before stirring until melted and smooth – if some lumps remain, microwave in 10-second bursts until completely melted and smooth.

3. Add the cream cheese, vanilla paste or extract, hazelnut butter, honey or maple syrup and salt and stir until smooth.

4. Pour into the prepared tin and smooth over the top. Drizzle with extra melted chocolate and sprinkle with the chopped hazelnuts.

5. Freeze for at least 4 hours, or until set.

6. Cut into 16–20 squares (or less if you're feeling extra indulgent) and enjoy!

CHOCOLATIER'S TIP
You can use a combination of thick kefir yogurt and cream cheese, if you prefer. You can try different flavour combinations for the decoration – why not take a look at our smooth EXCELLENCE Extra Creamy Milk Chocolate or sweet EXCELLENCE White Chocolate with a Touch of Vanilla?

STRAWBERRY AND CHOCOLATE CHEESECAKE PARFAIT

Try our chocolate twist on a classic fruity strawberry cheesecake featuring layers of crunchy biscuits, sweet vanilla-infused cream cheese, juicy strawberries and indulgent LINDOR Truffles. Spoons at the ready!

SERVES: 2
PREP: 20 mins + chilling

150g strawberries
160ml double cream
30g icing sugar, sifted
2 tsp vanilla extract
125g full-fat cream
    cheese, at room
    temperature
7 **LINDOR Double**
    Chocolate Truffles,
    unwrapped (see Tip)
50g digestives, blitzed
    into crumbs (see Tip)
15g butter, melted

1. Hull the strawberries and chop into small pieces. Tip into a small bowl and set aside.

2. In a large bowl, whip the cream and icing sugar with 1 teaspoon of the vanilla extract until soft peaks form.

3. In a separate bowl, beat the cream cheese until smooth. Gradually beat into the whipped cream mix until combined.

4. Chop 5 LINDOR Double Chocolate Truffles into quarters and tip them into a separate bowl.

5. In another bowl, combine the blitzed biscuits, melted butter and remaining teaspoon of vanilla extract.

6. Set out 2 tumbler glasses. Add one-sixth of the cream mix to the bottom of each glass. Top with a layer of biscuit crumbs, followed by the chopped strawberries and the chopped LINDOR Truffles. Repeat so that you have 3 layers of cream mix and 2 layers of strawberries, chopped truffles and biscuits.

7. Finish each with a whole LINDOR Truffle. Chill until ready to serve.

CHOCOLATIER'S TIP
If you prefer a sweeter chocolate, substitute the LINDOR Double Chocolate Truffles for our delicate LINDOR Strawberries & Cream. You can make this recipe gluten free by using gluten-free biscuits. If making this recipe for someone following a gluten-free diet, always check the manufacturer's label to ensure your ingredients are free from gluten.

LINDOR SURPRISE CUPCAKES

Take your classic cupcake recipe to the next level by adding a hidden smooth melting LINDOR chocolate centre. Perfect for any occasion.

MAKES: 12
PREP: 25 mins + chilling
COOK: 25 mins

FOR THE CUPCAKES:
160g plain flour
50g cocoa powder
1 tsp baking powder
½ tsp bicarbonate of soda
Pinch of salt
2 large eggs
125ml sunflower oil
225g caster sugar
50g soft light brown sugar
1 tsp vanilla extract
250ml buttermilk
24 **LINDOR Milk Truffles**
and **LINDOR White**
Truffles, unwrapped
(see Tip)

FOR THE CHOCOLATE
BUTTERCREAM:
100g **Lindt EXCELLENCE**
70% Dark Chocolate,
chopped
115g unsalted butter, at
room temperature
25g cocoa powder, sifted
185g icing sugar, sifted
3–4 tbsp double cream

1. Preheat the oven to 180°C/160°C Fan/Gas 4. Line a 12-hole muffin tin with paper cases and set aside.

2. Sift together the flour, cocoa powder, baking powder, bicarbonate of soda and salt, then set aside.

3. In a separate bowl, beat together the eggs, oil and sugars until light and fluffy. Beat in the vanilla extract.

4. Add the dry ingredients in batches, alternating with the buttermilk. Mix well to combine.

5. Spoon into the prepared cases until three-quarters full. Bake for 20–25 minutes or until a skewer inserted into the centre of the cake comes out clean. While still warm, press a LINDOR Milk Truffle into the centre of each cupcake. Leave to cool in the tin for 10 minutes before transferring to a wire rack to finish cooling completely.

6. For the chocolate buttercream: put the chopped chocolate in a heatproof bowl set over a pan of barely simmering water, ensuring the bottom of the bowl doesn't come into contact with the water, then stir until melted. Alternatively, pop the chocolate into a microwave-safe bowl and melt in 30-second bursts, stirring between each. Remove from the heat and leave to cool.

7. Beat the butter until pale and fluffy. Beat in the cooled melted chocolate until smooth. Beat in the cocoa powder and icing sugar, followed by the cream, until you have a smooth buttercream. Cover and chill for 10–15 minutes until thick enough to pipe.

8. Spoon into a piping bag and pipe swirls onto the cupcakes. To finish, add a LINDOR Truffle on top of each of the cupcakes.

Photograph overleaf →

CHOCOLATIER'S TIP
You can try different flavours of LINDOR in this recipe – try our LINDOR Hazelnut Truffles for an irresistibly nutty combination.

INDULGENT CHOCOLATE MILKSHAKE

Take this cooling classic to the next level with our decadent EXCELLENCE 70% Dark Chocolate. The perfect treat for a sunny summer's day.

SERVES: 4
PREP: 15 mins
COOK: 5 mins

FOR THE CHOCOLATE
   SAUCE:
175ml double cream
200g **Lindt EXCELLENCE**
   70% Dark Chocolate,
   finely chopped
25g unsalted butter,
   cut into cubes

FOR THE MILKSHAKE:
800ml milk
8 scoops of good-quality
   chocolate ice cream

TO DECORATE:
Whipped cream
Fresh cherries (see Tip)
Sprinkles

1. Make the chocolate sauce: put 4 tall glasses in the fridge to chill. Pour the cream into a saucepan until warm. Take off the heat and stir in the chopped chocolate until smooth and melted.

2. Gradually whisk in the butter until smooth and glossy. Pour into a jug or piping bag and set aside.

3. Prepare the milkshake: pour the milk into a blender, add the ice cream, and blitz until smooth.

4. Drizzle some of the chocolate sauce around the sides of the 4 tall chilled glasses (rotating the glass at an angle as you do this). Pour in the milkshake.

5. Top with whipped cream and drizzle with more of the chocolate sauce. Finish with a fresh cherry and sprinkles. Serve straight away.

CHOCOLATIER'S TIP
When in season, plump and juicy cherries add a wonderful burst of flavour to these decadent milkshakes. Swap for blueberries, strawberries, blackberries or raspberries depending on what is in season when you make these. You could also add a sprinkling of toasted nuts (chopped hazelnuts and almonds work well) for a bit of a crunch.

CHOCOLATE AND RASPBERRY PANCAKES

Take your brunch to the next level with these decadent chocolate and raspberry pancakes. You won't want to wait until the weekend...

SERVES: 4–6
PREP: 15 mins
COOK: 20 mins
   (depending on how
   many batches)

FOR THE PANCAKES:
250g self-raising flour
25g cocoa powder
2 tbsp caster sugar
2 eggs
Pinch of salt
300ml milk
Sunflower oil, for frying

TO SERVE:
150g **Lindt EXCELLENCE**
   Raspberry Intense Dark
   Chocolate, chopped
250ml double cream
25g icing sugar
250g raspberries
Lindt EXCELLENCE 70%
   Dark Chocolate, finely
   grated

1. Whisk the flour, cocoa powder and caster sugar together, then gradually whisk in the eggs, salt and milk until you have a smooth batter.

2. Meanwhile, put the chopped Lindt EXCELLENCE Raspberry Intense Dark Chocolate in a heatproof bowl and set it over a pan of barely simmering water, ensuring the bottom of the bowl doesn't come into contact with the water, then stir until melted. Alternatively, pop the chocolate into a microwave-safe bowl and melt in 30-second bursts, stirring between each. Remove from the heat and leave to cool for 5 minutes, then pour into a jug.

3. Whip the cream with the icing sugar using an electric whisk until stiff peaks form, taking care not to over-whip. Set aside.

4. Brush a nonstick frying pan with a little sunflower oil and place over a medium heat. Once the pan is hot, put 2 tablespoons of batter into the pan and gently spread out to form a small disc. Leave to cook for 1–2 minutes or until bubbles start to form – don't be tempted to fiddle with it. Flip using a palette knife or spatula and cook for a further minute or so until just firm.

5. Continue to cook the pancakes in batches, brushing the pan with a little more oil as needed.

6. Serve the pancakes with a dollop of whipped cream, a drizzle of melted EXCELLENCE Raspberry Intense Dark Chocolate, a sprinkling of fresh raspberries and grated dark chocolate. Serve any remaining melted chocolate and whipped cream on the side.

CHOCOLATIER'S TIP
To make these extra special, pipe the whipped cream on top using a piping bag fitted with a star nozzle.

CROISSANT BAKED FRENCH TOAST

Looking for a delicious breakfast, brunch or pudding for a special occasion? Our Master Chocolatiers have weaved their magic on the ever-popular French toast to create this irresistible recipe. Imagine buttery croissants filled with our rich and decadent chocolate spread, baked in an indulgent custard. It is sure to become your go-to celebration recipe.

SERVES: 4
PREP: 10 mins + soaking
COOK: 30 mins

4 croissants, one day old
4 heaped tbsp **Lindt Dark Chocolate Spread**
4 tbsp chopped hazelnuts
300ml double cream
2 large eggs
50g caster sugar
2 tbsp demerara sugar
50g **Lindt EXCELLENCE 70% Dark Chocolate**, roughly chopped

TO SERVE (OPTIONAL):
Lightly whipped cream
1 tbsp chopped hazelnuts
Lindt Dark Chocolate Spread
Fresh berries

1. Preheat the oven to 180°C/160°C Fan/Gas 4. Set aside a 18 x 25 x 5cm deep ovenproof dish (it should accommodate your croissants snuggly).

2. Slice the croissants in half down the centre, horizontally – take care not to go all the way through as you need to keep the edges intact.

3. Spread 1 generously heaped tbsp of Lindt Dark Chocolate Spread into the centre of each croissant, then sprinkle with half of the hazelnuts and then sandwich together. Arrange the croissants, overlapping slightly in the dish.

4. In a small bowl, whisk together the cream, eggs and caster sugar until combined.

5. Pour the cream mixture over the croissants, ensuring all are equally covered. Leave to soak for 10 minutes.

6. Sprinkle the remaining hazelnuts, the demerara sugar and chopped chocolate over the top of the croissants.

7. Transfer the dish into the oven and bake for about 30 minutes – or until golden brown and bubbling round the edges and in the centre. You should be able to see the custard has cooked through.

8. Remove from the oven. Spoon into bowls and serve with lightly whipped cream, an extra sprinkling of chopped hazelnuts, extra Lindt Dark Chocolate Spread and fresh berries, if wished.

CHOCOLATIER'S TIP
You can adjust the recipe to suit your tastes; try using our Lindt Hazelnut Chocolate Spread instead of our Lindt Dark Chocolate Spread, or swap the hazelnuts for chopped almonds or pistachios.

CHOCOLATE FRUIT BOUQUET

This has to be one of the best ways to reach your 5-a-day! What could be more delicious than ripe and juicy fruit, dipped in our luxurious Swiss chocolate, arranged in a beautiful bouquet?

MAKES: 25 fruit skewers
PREP: 25 mins + chilling

250g **Lindt EXCELLENCE 70% Dark Chocolate**, or **Lindt COOKING 70% Dark Intense,** chopped
25 fresh strawberries, hulled
Slices of pineapple or melon
Physalis, leaves removed

TO DECORATE:
Freeze-dried raspberries
Toasted coconut flakes, chopped, or desiccated coconut
Shelled pistachios, chopped

TO ASSEMBLE:
A flower cookie cutter
25 thin skewers
1 orange

1. Line a baking sheet with greaseproof paper and set aside.

2. Put the chopped chocolate in a heatproof bowl set over a pan of barely simmering water, ensuring the bottom of the bowl doesn't come into contact with the water, then stir until melted. Alternatively, pop the chocolate into a microwave-safe bowl and melt in 30-second bursts, stirring between each. Remove from the heat and leave to cool.

3. Dip the pointed end of strawberries into the cooled melted chocolate and place them pointed side up onto the prepared baking sheet – you may wish to leave some strawberries plain for variety.

4. Sprinkle with your choice of: freeze-dried raspberries, chopped toasted coconut flakes or dessicated coconut and chopped pistachios. Leave to set (you can chill in the fridge for 10–15 minutes to speed up the process).

5. Meanwhile, using a flower cookie cutter, stamp out 25 flowers from the pineapple or melon slices. Slide onto the thin skewers and top with a physalis.

6. Place the orange in the base of a large mug.

7. Poke a skewer into the orange and top with a strawberry. Repeat with the remaining skewers and strawberries.

CHOCOLATIER'S TIP
We have used our EXCELLENCE 70% Dark Chocolate which is vegan-friendly (so are our EXCELLENCE 85%, 90% and 99% Dark Chocolate Bars) but take a look at our extensive range of luxurious Swiss milk and white chocolates – they all pair perfectly with the freshest fruit.

DARK CHOCOLATE AND MINT POPSICLES

Cool down with these refreshing popsicles made using the finest dark chocolate infused with peppermint oil. These are an irresistible treat on a scorching summer's day.

MAKES: 6 x 90ml popsicles
PREP: 10 mins + freezing
COOK: 5 mins

325ml semi-skimmed milk
150g **Lindt EXCELLENCE Intense Mint Dark Chocolate**, chopped

1. Pour half of the milk into a large saucepan and add the chopped chocolate. Heat over a medium-low heat, stirring all the time, until the chocolate has melted and you have a smooth and velvety chocolate milk mix.

2. Gradually add the remaining milk, stirring all the time, until you have a smooth chocolate milk. Remove from the heat and set aside to cool.

3. Once the chocolate milk has cooled, divide equally between six 90ml popsicle moulds. Top with the lids and insert the popsicle sticks. Freeze until frozen (at least 6 hours).

4. To unmould the mint chocolate popsicles: fill a deep pan with hot water (it needs to be as deep as the height of the moulds). Dip the moulds in the hot water just long enough to release the popsicles whilst gently pulling on the stick. Serve straight away (see Tip).

CHOCOLATIER'S TIP
For double-chocolate popsicles, after removing these from their moulds, dip the ends in melted EXCELLENCE 70% Dark Chocolate and chill to set the chocolate layer before serving.

CHOCOLATE MARSHMALLOW RICE POP SQUARES

The Lindt Master Chocolatiers have combined juicy dried cranberries and intense EXCELLENCE 85% Dark Chocolate to balance out the sweetness of the marshmallows and EXCELLENCE White Chocolate with a Touch of Vanilla in these sweet and crispy squares – topped off with EXCELLENCE 70% Dark Chocolate for an extra layer of luxury.

MAKES: 16
PREP: 15 mins + cooling
COOK: 15 mins

100g unsalted butter, diced, plus extra for greasing
100g mini marshmallows
100g **Lindt EXCELLENCE White Chocolate with a Touch of Vanilla**, finely chopped
150g rice pop cereal
75g dried cranberries
75g **Lindt EXCELLENCE 85% Dark Chocolate**, roughly chopped

TO DECORATE:
200g **Lindt EXCELLENCE 70% Dark Chocolate**, chopped

1. Grease and line a 20cm deep, loose-bottomed square tin with greaseproof paper.

2. In a non-stick saucepan, melt the butter, marshmallows and chopped white chocolate over a low heat, stirring until melted and smooth. It may split slightly but will come together when whisking.

3. Remove from the heat and leave to cool for 2 minutes. Stir in the rice pops, followed by the dried cranberries and chopped Lindt EXCELLENCE 85% Dark Chocolate until completely coated in the chocolate-marshmallow mix (it will be sticky). Don't worry, some of the dark chocolate will melt slightly.

4. Tip into the prepared tin and smooth in an even layer using the back of a spoon. Set aside.

5. Put the chopped Lindt EXCELLENCE 70% Dark Chocolate in a heatproof bowl set over a pan of barely simmering water, ensuring the bottom of the bowl doesn't come into contact with the water, then stir until melted. Alternatively, pop into a microwave-safe bowl and melt in 30-second bursts, stirring between each.

6. Remove the bowl from the heat and pour over the rice pop-marshmallow mix. Use the back of a spoon to spread in a smooth layer and shake slightly so it's even. Leave to cool completely in a cool, dry place for at least 3 hours, or until set. Remove from the tin and set onto a plate before cutting into 16 squares (see Tip).

CHOCOLATIER'S TIP
Run a sharp knife under boiling water and dry thoroughly before cutting – this will help you slice it into squares easily.

DARK CHOCOLATE ALMOND BARK

Crunchy almonds enrobed in the finest Swiss dark chocolate – perfect for
a homemade gift at any time of the year. Plus, it is vegan-friendly!

MAKES: 1 large slab
PREP: 15 mins + cooling

400g **Lindt EXCELLENCE
70% Dark Chocolate**,
or **Lindt COOKING
70% Dark Intense,**
chopped
150g almonds (see Tip)

1. Line a large baking sheet with greaseproof paper and set aside.

2. Put the chopped chocolate in a heatproof bowl set over a pan
   of barely simmering water, ensuring the bottom of the bowl
   doesn't come into contact with the water, then stir until melted.
   Alternatively, pop the chocolate into a microwave-safe bowl and
   melt in 30-second bursts, stirring between each. Remove from
   the heat and leave to cool.

3. Add the almonds and stir until completely coated.

4. Pour over the prepared baking sheet and, using a palette knife, spread
   into a large rectangle (about the size of an A4 sheet of paper).

5. Leave to set in a cool place (you can chill in the fridge to speed
   up the process but the chocolate may lose its gloss).

6. Break into shards (or leave as a giant slab) and wrap in pretty
   cellophane bags before tying with ribbons. Enjoy within 2 weeks.

CHOCOLATIER'S TIP
Ring the changes by swapping the almonds for hazelnuts or
substituting half for plump and juicy raisins.

HOSTING

MIXED BERRY PAVLOVA

Pavlovas are stunning centrepiece desserts – ideal for parties and celebrations. This recipe, featuring our decadent EXCELLENCE 70% Dark Chocolate, is perfect to make during cherry season.

SERVES: 8–10
PREP: 40 mins + cooling
COOK: 1 hour 40 mins

6 large egg whites, at
    room temperature
350g caster sugar
2 tsp fresh lemon juice
2 tsp cornflour
1 tsp vanilla extract

TO DECORATE:
175g **Lindt EXCELLENCE
    70% Dark Chocolate**,
    chopped, plus 1 square
350ml double cream
2 tbsp icing sugar
1 tsp vanilla extract
2 tsp freeze-dried
    raspberries
450g fresh cherries and
    mixed berries (see Tip)

CHOCOLATIER'S TIP
Our Lindt Master
Chocolatiers recommend
using the most seasonal
fruits for this recipe. If
serving to children, make
sure you destone the
cherries before plating up.

1. Preheat the oven to 130°C/110°C Fan/Gas ½. Draw a large 20cm circle on a sheet of greaseproof paper, turn over (so the markings are facing down) and place on a large baking tray.

2. Tip the egg whites into the bowl of an electric mixer and whisk on medium speed until white and stiff (when you turn the bowl upside down, they should hold their shape).

3. Gradually add the sugar with the whisk still running. Be patient and do this step slowly, it can take up to 15 minutes. Continue whisking until you have a stiff and glossy meringue.

4. Add the lemon juice, cornflour and vanilla extract. Whisk for 2 minutes to combine.

5. Using a spatula, scrape the meringue mixture onto the prepared baking tray, piling it into the centre. Carefully spread around the edges to form a large circle, lifting upwards to create a tall dome shape.

6. Bake in the oven for 10 minutes before reducing the temperature to 90°C/70°C Fan/Gas ¼ and cooking for a further 1 hour 30 minutes. Turn off the oven and leave to cool completely inside for at least 2 hours (the slower it cools, the less likely the risk of the meringue cracking).

7. Once the pavlova has cooled, put the chopped chocolate in a heatproof bowl set over a pan of barely simmering water, ensuring the bottom of the bowl doesn't come into contact with the water, then stir until melted. Alternatively, pop the chocolate into a microwave-safe bowl and melt in 30-second bursts, stirring between each.

8. In a medium bowl, whip the cream with the icing sugar and vanilla extract until you have medium peaks.

9. Set the cooled pavlova onto a flat plate. Top with the whipped cream and sprinkle with freeze-dried raspberries. Arrange the cherries and mixed berries on top. Drizzle with most of the melted chocolate and nestle in a square of Lindt EXCELLENCE 70% Dark Chocolate. Serve straight away with any remaining melted chocolate on the side.

MILK CHOCOLATE TRUFFLES

Discover our sumptuous, smooth and irresistibly creamy Lindt GOLD BAR Milk Chocolate – ideal for making these delicious milk chocolate truffles. The perfect gift for friends... or for treating yourself.

MAKES: 20–30
PREP: 35 mins + chilling
COOK: 5 mins

300g **GOLD BAR Milk Chocolate**, chopped
250ml double cream
15g butter, at room temperature

TO DECORATE:
Desiccated coconut
Finely chopped Lindt chocolate of your choice
Cocoa powder
Finely chopped nuts

1. Put the chopped chocolate into a heatproof bowl and set aside.

2. Pour the cream into a saucepan and bring to the boil. Remove from the heat and pour it over the chopped chocolate. Add the butter and stir until melted and you have a smooth milk chocolate ganache. Leave to cool completely before covering and chilling in the fridge for 5 hours, preferably overnight or until firm enough to shape.

3. Line separate plates with greaseproof paper and cover with your chosen decorations.

4. Using a melon baller, small ice cream scoop or teaspoon, scoop the ganache into a small ball.

5. Use your fingertips to quickly and gently roll into a smooth ball (see Tip).

6. Roll in your chosen decorations to coat, before setting onto a plate. Repeat until you have used up all the ganache (you should have 20–30 truffles).

7. Set onto a flat plate, cover and chill in the fridge until ready to serve.

CHOCOLATIER'S TIP
When shaping, try to handle the truffles as little as possible, as the heat of your palms will cause them to melt.

CHOCOLATE ORANGE CHEESECAKE

This opulent cheesecake takes chocolate orange to a whole new level. Our delicious EXCELLENCE Orange Intense – featuring delicate orange pieces and toasted almonds enrobed in the finest dark chocolate – creates a wonderfully rich and zesty filling. Serve 'au natural' or top with slices of candied orange and curls of dark chocolate for added 'wow factor'.

SERVES: 10–12
PREP: 35 mins + chilling
COOK: 1 hour 15 mins

FOR THE BASE:
150g unsalted butter, melted, plus extra for greasing
250g digestives
A couple of drops of vanilla extract

FOR THE FILLING:
575g full-fat cream cheese, at room temperature
60g full-fat sour cream
130g caster sugar, plus 1 tbsp
100ml orange juice
200g **Lindt EXCELLENCE Orange Intense Dark Chocolate**, melted
4 eggs

1. For the base: preheat the oven to 160°C/140°C Fan/Gas 3. Grease a deep 23cm springform tin with butter and line the base with baking paper. It's easiest to unclip the ring, put the baking paper over the base and clip the ring back. Wrap the bottom of the tin with a double layer of foil (this helps ensure against water leaking into the crust while baking the cheesecake in a hot water bath). Place into a large deep roasting tin and set aside.

2. Blitz together the digestives and vanilla extract in a processor until finely ground. Add the melted butter and blitz until you have the consistency of damp sand.

3. Tip into the base of the prepared tin and spread over with the back of a spoon until you have a flat and even layer.

4. For the filling: using an electric mixer, beat the cream cheese until smooth, scraping down the side of the bowl occasionally. Add the sour cream and sugar and beat until smooth and combined.

5. Add the orange juice to the cream cheese and beat until combined, scraping down the sides of the bowl occasionally. Then pour in the melted chocolate while whisking.

6. Add the eggs, one at a time, mixing until just incorporated – you should have a smooth and creamy mix.

7. Spoon the cheesecake mixture over the biscuit base, smoothing the top with a back of the spoon.

CHOCOLATIER'S TIP
Don't be tempted to skip the water bath, it creates a beautiful texture that makes all the difference in a cheesecake.

TO DECORATE:

2 squares **Lindt EXCELLENCE 70% Dark Chocolate**, grated

Pared zest of 1 orange

8. Transfer the roasting tin to the oven and pour enough hot water into the tin to come halfway up the side of the springform tin.

9. Bake for 1 hour–1 hour 15 minutes, or until the side of the cake is set but the centre is still slightly soft.

10. Remove from the water bath, run a palette knife around the rim, and leave to cool completely. Then chill for at least 6 hours in the fridge.

11. Remove from the tin and set onto a flat serving plate. Decorate with a grating of chocolate and orange zest and then slice using a hot knife.

CHOCOLATE PANNA COTTA WITH PISTACHIO SAUCE

A celebration of Italian flavours! Think rich EXCELLENCE 70% Dark Chocolate and Amaretto-infused panna cotta with a nutty pistachio sauce.

MAKES: 6
PREP: 20 mins + chilling
COOK: 20 mins

FOR THE CHOCOLATE
  PANNA COTTA:
Vegetable oil, for greasing
3 sheets of gelatine
400ml double cream
2–3 tbsp Amaretto liqueur
75g icing sugar
Pinch of salt
100g **Lindt EXCELLENCE**
  70% Dark Chocolate,
  chopped

FOR THE PISTACHIO
  SAUCE:
125ml full-fat milk
125ml double cream
50g caster sugar
3 egg yolks
60g peeled pistachios

FOR THE CARAMELISED
  PISTACHIOS:
3 tbsp runny honey
2 tbsp water
100g peeled pistachios,
  toasted

1. Lightly oil 6 heatproof moulds. We like to use 90ml silicon moulds.

2. Soak the gelatine leaves in a bowl of cold water for 5 minutes. Make sure the leaves are fully submerged in water.

3. Put the cream, Amaretto, icing sugar and salt into a saucepan, and slowly bring to a simmer, then immediately remove from the heat. Stir in the chopped chocolate until smooth and melted.

4. Squeeze the excess water from the gelatine and stir into the chocolate cream until dissolved.

5. If using silicon moulds, place on a tray so the moulds are steady when you move them to the fridge. Pour your panna cotta mixture into the prepared moulds and leave to cool completely, before covering and chilling for at least 4 hours (or until set).

6. Meanwhile, make the pistachio sauce: whisk together the milk, cream, caster sugar and egg yolks in a saucepan over a low-medium heat until thick and creamy.

7. Pour into a blender, add the pistachios, and blitz until smooth. Leave to cool completely before covering and chilling in the fridge, bringing up to room temperature before using.

8. Pour the honey and water into a frying pan. Bring to a boil and simmer for 1–2 minutes until thick and golden. Add the pistachios, stir to coat and cook for 1–2 minutes until sticky and the honey has reduced. Spread in an even layer on a tray lined with baking paper.

9. To unmould the panna cottas, fill a deep heatproof bowl with hot water. Briefly dip the moulds into the water to loosen. Turn out onto a flat plate. Pour over the chilled pistachio sauce and sprinkle over the caramelised pistachios. Serve immediately.

CHOCOLATIER'S TIP
If you prefer, sprinkle with caramelised hazelnuts instead of pistachios.

LINDOR TRUFFLE TIRAMISU

Add a little Lindt luxury to an Italian classic to create this show-stopping dessert featuring layers of coffee-infused ladyfinger biscuits, sweet cream and silky LINDOR Truffles.

SERVES: 6
PREP: 25 mins + chilling

300ml freshly brewed
  strong coffee, cooled
3 tbsp rum
250ml double cream
350g mascarpone
50g caster sugar
2 tsp vanilla extract
3 tbsp Amaretto liqueur
125g ladyfingers (see Tip)
1–2 squares of **Lindt**
  EXCELLENCE 70%
  Dark Chocolate
7 **LINDOR 70% Dark**
  Truffles, unwrapped and
  quartered

TO DECORATE:
18 **LINDOR Milk Truffles**,
  unwrapped and halved
  (see Tip)
Cocoa powder, for dusting

CHOCOLATIER'S TIP
The exact number of
truffles and ladyfingers will
depend on the size, and
shape, of your dish.

1. Mix together the coffee and rum in a shallow bowl and set aside.

2. In a large bowl, whisk the double cream until you have soft peaks. Set aside.

3. In a separate bowl, beat the mascarpone with the sugar, vanilla extract and Amaretto liqueur for about 2 minutes or until smooth. Fold in the whipped cream until you have a smooth and creamy mix.

4. Dip half of the ladyfingers, one at a time, into the coffee mixture. Ensure that both sides are soaked but do not stay in long enough to disintegrate (you want them to absorb the flavour but still stay intact – the colour should change slightly and they should soften a little).

5. Layer the soaked ladyfingers into the base of a 1.25 L deep dish (ours was around 18 x 18 x 5cm) – you may need to break a couple of the biscuits to fit snugly or dip extra to cover the base.

6. Top with half of the mascarpone mix, smoothing over with the back of a spoon in an even layer to completely cover the biscuits.

7. Using a fine grater, grate over the Lindt EXCELLENCE 70% Dark Chocolate square to cover the surface (you may need 2 depending on the shape of your dish). Scatter over the quartered LINDOR 60% Dark Truffles in an even layer.

8. Soak the remaining ladyfingers and add on top (dipping extra if required). Top with the remaining mascarpone mixture, smoothing the top as before. Decorate with the halved LINDOR Milk Truffles, cut side facing down, and dust with cocoa powder. Cover and chill for at least 6 hours, or overnight.

9. Serve chilled or, if you prefer, remove from the fridge 30 minutes before serving to allow it to come to room temperature.

MILK CHOCOLATE CRÈME BRÛLÉE

An indulgent chocolate version of this classic custard dessert, made using
our luxuriously mellow EXCELLENCE Extra Creamy Milk Chocolate.

MAKES: 8
PREP: 20 mins + chilling
COOK: 1 hour

1 L double cream
200g **Lindt EXCELLENCE**
  Extra Creamy Milk
  Chocolate, finely
  chopped
8 large egg yolks
150g caster sugar

TO DECORATE:
Around 8–12 tsp
  caster sugar
Fresh raspberries

1. Preheat the oven to 150°C/130°C Fan/Gas 2. Place a rack in the centre of the oven. Put eight 175ml ramekins into a large roasting tin.

2. Pour the cream into a large saucepan and heat gently until simmering. Add the chopped chocolate and stir until melted and smooth. Remove from the heat.

3. In a large heatproof bowl, whisk the egg yolks with the caster sugar until the sugar dissolves and the mixture is smooth. Whisk in 2 tablespoons of the hot chocolate cream mixture.

4. Slowly drizzle the remaining cream mixture into the whisked egg yolks, whisking continuously.

5. Strain the chocolate mixture through a fine sieve into a large heatproof jug. Pour into the ramekins.

6. Transfer the roasting tin with the ramekins into the oven. Pour enough hot water into the tin to come halfway up the side of the ramekins. Bake for around 50 minutes, or until the edges are set (but not brown) and the centre has a slight wobble.

7. Remove the ramekins from the roasting tin and pat dry. Leave to cool completely before covering with cling film and chilling for at least 3 hours, or overnight.

8. To serve: around 30 minutes before serving, remove the crème brûlées from the fridge and take off the cling film. Sprinkle each with around 1½ teaspoons of caster sugar (or enough to evenly cover the top of the ramekin). Using a mini kitchen blowtorch, working on one ramekin at a time, caramelise the sugar until it melts and turns dark amber. Leave to cool for 5 minutes before sprinkling with fresh raspberries and serving.

CHOCOLATIER'S TIP
Use your leftover egg whites to make meringues or a pavlova
(see page 108).

MINI DARK CHOCOLATE AND RASPBERRY CHEESECAKES

The old adage 'all good things come in small packages' is spot on
for these dainty desserts! Delve into decadence with three tiers of
indulgence: a crushed digestive biscuit base, topped with smooth
chocolate cheesecake, finished with a gloriously glossy ganache.
Treat your guests, your loved ones – or yourself...

MAKES: 6 cheesecakes
PREP: 20 mins + chilling
COOK: 25 mins

FOR THE BASE:
1 tbsp unsalted butter,
    melted, plus extra for
    greasing
75g chocolate digestives,
    blitzed into crumbs

FOR THE FILLING:
125g full-fat cream
    cheese, at room
    temperature
30g caster sugar
1 large egg
50g **Lindt EXCELLENCE**
    Raspberry Intense Dark
    Chocolate, melted and
    cooled

1. Preheat the oven to 180°C/160°C Fan/Gas 4. Grease six x 65ml
   heart or round silicone moulds, you can also use a large muffin tin
   with cases or different-shaped moulds.

2. Mix together the blitzed chocolate digestives and melted butter
   in a bowl until you have the consistency of damp sand.

3. Divide evenly between the prepared moulds (around 1 tablespoon
   each). Press firmly into the bottom using your fingers or the back
   of a teaspoon, until you have a smooth and even layer. Bake for
   8 minutes. Set aside to cool.

4. For the cheesecake filling: beat the cream cheese with the caster
   sugar until well combined. Scrape down the sides of the bowl and
   add the egg, beating well. Drizzle in the melted chocolate and mix
   to combine.

5. Pop the silicone moulds onto a baking sheet and carefully divide
   the cheesecake filling between them. Smooth over the surface.

6. Bake for 12–15 minutes or until the centres are just set but still have
   a slight wobble. Remove from the oven and leave to cool completely
   before covering and chilling in the fridge for at least 3 hours (or
   overnight). You can also put them in the freezer to make them
   easier to come out of the moulds.

7. When you are ready to serve, make the glaze. Pop the finely
   chopped chocolate in a heatproof bowl and set aside. Pour the
   cream into a small saucepan and slowly bring to a simmer. Remove
   from the heat and pour over the chopped chocolate. Whisk gently
   until all the chocolate has melted and you have a smooth, glossy
   glaze. Leave to stand for 3 minutes.

FOR THE CHOCOLATE
  GLAZE:
50g **Lindt EXCELLENCE
  70% Dark Chocolate**,
  finely chopped (see Tip)
4 tbsp double cream

TO DECORATE:
Freeze-dried raspberries,
  fresh raspberries,
  sprinkles or edible
  flowers (optional)

8. Carefully pop the cheesecakes out of their moulds and set onto flat plates. Spoon 1–2 tablespoons chocolate glaze on top and pour any remaining glaze into small pots to serve on the side. Leave to defrost if needed.

9. Sprinkle with freeze-dried raspberries, fresh raspberries, sprinkles or edible flower petals, if desired, and serve.

TIP: If you have 125ml moulds then simply double the recipe.

Photograph overleaf →

CHOCOLATIER'S TIP
You can swap our luxurious Lindt EXCELLENCE 70% Dark Chocolate for our Lindt EXCELLENCE Raspberry Intense Dark Chocolate to heighten the fruity raspberry flavour.

CHOCOLATE SOUFFLÉS

These luxurious soufflés are perfect for a special occasion pudding.
Imagine individual decadent, fluffy, dark chocolate cakes … pure
chocolate heaven.

MAKES: 2
PREP: 5 mins
COOK: 20 mins

Spray oil, for greasing
60g **Lindt EXCELLENCE
70% Dark Chocolate**,
chopped
30g unsalted butter
20g caster sugar
2 large eggs
2 tbsp plain flour
Pinch of fine sea salt
2 squares of **Lindt
EXCELLENCE 70%
Dark Chocolate**

TO SERVE (OPTIONAL):
Whipped cream, ice
cream or yogurt
Fresh raspberries
Edible dried rose petals
(see Tip)

1. Preheat the oven to 190°C/170°C Fan/Gas 5. Spray two x 175ml dariole moulds or ramekins with spray oil.

2. Place the chopped chocolate with the butter into a heatproof bowl set over a pan of barely simmering water, ensuring the bottom of the bowl doesn't come into contact with the water, then stir until melted. Alternatively, pop into a microwave-safe bowl and melt in 30-second bursts, stirring between each. Remove from the heat and leave to cool.

3. Whisk in the sugar and eggs, followed by the flour and salt.

4. Add 2 tablespoons of the chocolate mixture into each of the prepared moulds. Top each with a square of chocolate. Divide the remaining mix over the chocolate squares to cover.

5. Bake in the oven for 10–14 minutes or until risen and the top is cooked.

6. Serve immediately with your choice of whipped cream, ice cream or yogurt, fresh raspberries and edible dried rose petals, if wished.

CHOCOLATIER'S TIP
The rose petals add a beautiful burst of colour and subtle floral fragrance. You can, of course, omit them, if wished.

COCONUT AND PASSIONFRUIT MACARONS

Sweet coconut macarons filled with a creamy double chocolate and passionfruit filling – a tempting tropical treat which is perfect for summer!

MAKES: about 25
PREP: 35 mins + setting
COOK: 20 mins

125g desiccated coconut
210g icing sugar
1 tbsp cocoa powder
3 egg whites
30g caster sugar

FOR THE FILLING:
4 passionfruits
75ml double cream
50g caster sugar
100g **Lindt EXCELLENCE 70% Dark Chocolate**, finely chopped (see Tip)
100g **Lindt EXCELLENCE Extra Creamy Milk Chocolate**, finely chopped (see Tip)

1. Preheat the oven to 170°C/150°C Fan/Gas 3. Line 2 large flat baking sheets with greaseproof paper.

2. Blitz the desiccated coconut, icing sugar and cocoa powder in a blender until as finely ground as possible.

3. In a separate bowl, whisk the egg whites with the caster sugar until stiff.

4. Gently fold the blitzed coconut mix into the whisked egg whites, taking care to keep in as much air as possible.

5. Spoon into a piping bag fitted with a plain round nozzle and pipe same-sized circles (approximately 3cm in diameter), a few centimetres apart, onto the prepared baking sheets. Leave to dry for 30 minutes.

6. Bake for about 15 minutes or until just firm to touch. Leave to cool on the baking sheets.

7. For the filling: halve the passionfruits and scrape out the pulp into a saucepan. Add the cream and sugar and bring to the boil, stirring often.

8. Remove from the heat and push through a sieve into a heatproof bowl. Stir in the chopped chocolate until melted and smooth. Leave to cool completely.

9. Spoon the passionfruit-chocolate cream into a piping bag fitted with a small nozzle and pipe a small amount onto half of the cooled macarons. Top with a macaron top and set onto a flat plate.

CHOCOLATIER'S TIP

For a more intense chocolate filling, use 200g of our EXCELLENCE 70% Dark Chocolate instead of half and half. If making this recipe for someone following a gluten-free diet, always check the manufacturer's label to ensure all your ingredients are free from gluten.

SPICED DARK CHOCOLATE DISCS

These subtly spiced, vegan-friendly, dark chocolate discs are ideal for
a little chocolate indulgence. They also make perfect presents when
wrapped in pretty cellophane bags.

MAKES: about 25
PREP: 20 mins + chilling

300g **Lindt EXCELLENCE
70% Dark Chocolate**,
chopped

FOR THE TOPPINGS
(OPTIONAL):
3 tbsp blanched nuts,
chopped
1 tsp chilli flakes
1 tsp flaked sea salt
Zest of 1 large orange
2 tbsp sesame seeds

1. Line 2 baking sheets with greaseproof paper.

2. Put the chopped chocolate in a heatproof bowl set over a pan
   of barely simmering water, ensuring the bottom of the bowl
   doesn't come into contact with the water, then stir until melted.
   Alternatively, pop the chocolate into a microwave-safe bowl and
   melt in 30-second bursts, stirring between each. Remove from the
   heat and leave to cool.

3. Pour 1–2 tablespoon rounds of the melted chocolate, spaced apart,
   onto the prepared baking sheets. Carefully spread, using the back
   of a spoon, to form discs about 5–6cm in diameter.

4. Sprinkle over your choice of toppings and leave to set in the fridge
   for 20–30 minutes.

CHOCOLATIER'S TIP
You can experiment with different-flavoured discs; for a fruity twist,
sprinkle with freeze-dried raspberries or take inspiration from the
tropics and add a sprinkling of desiccated coconut. If making this
recipe for someone following a gluten-free diet, always check the
manufacturer's label to ensure your ingredients are free from gluten.

FESTIVE

EASTER CHOCOLATE CARROT CAKE

This deliciously moist, refreshingly zesty carrot cake is the perfect alternative to a traditional Simnel cake – decorated with a smooth cream cheese frosting and a luxurious Lindt chocolate drizzle.

SERVES: 12–14
PREP: 1 hour + cooling and chilling
COOK: 1 hour

FOR THE CARROT CAKE:
300ml vegetable oil, plus extra for greasing
200g full-fat Greek yogurt
4 eggs
Grated zest of 4 oranges
200g caster sugar
200g soft light brown sugar
400g carrots, tops cut off and coarsely grated
500g self-raising flour
4 tsp ground cinnamon

FOR THE CHOCOLATE DRIZZLE:
90ml double cream
20g golden syrup
90g **Lindt EXCELLENCE 70% Dark Chocolate**, chopped
20g unsalted butter

Ingredients continued overleaf →

1. For the cake: preheat the oven to 180°C/160°C Fan/Gas 4. Grease and line three 20cm round sandwich tins with baking paper.

2. Whisk the yogurt, oil, eggs and orange zest together. In a separate bowl combine the sugars, carrots, flour and cinnamon.

3. Gradually stir the wet ingredients into the dry until you have a smooth batter.

4. Divide the batter between the prepared tins and bake for 50–55 minutes until the cake is golden on top and a skewer inserted into the centre comes out clean. Leave to cool in the tins for 10 minutes, then turn out onto a wire rack to cool completely.

5. To make the drizzle: pour the cream into a saucepan, add the golden syrup, and slowly bring to a simmer. Stir in the chopped chocolate, followed by the butter, until smooth, melted and glossy. Pour into a heatproof bowl and set aside to cool.

6. For the cream cheese frosting: using an electric mixer, whisk the butter and cream cheese together until soft. Then add in the icing sugar and vanilla extract and whisk until the frosting is smooth and thick.

Method continued overleaf →

EASTER CHOCOLATE CARROT CAKE *continued*

FOR THE CREAM CHEESE
  FROSTING:
100g unsalted butter,
  at room temperature
425g full-fat cream
  cheese, at room
  temperature
150g icing sugar
1 tsp vanilla extract

TO DECORATE:
Lindt Easter Chocolates
  (such as **Mini LINDOR
  Eggs**, **Lindt GOLD
  BUNNY Minis** and our
  classic **Lindt GOLD
  BUNNY**), unwrapped

7. To assemble: place the first cake onto a flat plate. Top with a
    quarter of the frosting and spread it in an even layer. Repeat with
    the second cake and another layer of frosting before topping with
    the final cake. Use the remaining frosting to cover the top and sides
    of the cake – a palette knife will help create a smooth and even
    layer. Allow to chill for 15 minutes in the fridge.

8. Spread the chocolate drizzle on the top and sides of the cake.
    Arrange your choice of Lindt Easter chocolates (see Tip) over
    the top.

CHOCOLATIER'S TIP
Every Easter our Lindt Master Chocolatiers conjure up a range of
luxurious Swiss chocolate Easter creations. You can also make
this throughout the year and decorate with our irresistably smooth
LINDOR Truffles.

LINDOR EASTER EGG POPS

If you are looking for a fun activity during the Easter holidays, why not try these delicious LINDOR Easter Egg Pops? Imagine creamy LINDOR Chocolate Eggs encased in a sweet coating of our EXCELLENCE White Chocolate with a Touch of Vanilla and your choice of sugar sprinkles. Get creative and release your inner artist!

MAKES: 12
PREP: 30 mins + cooling

200g **Lindt EXCELLENCE White Chocolate with a Touch of Vanilla**, chopped
12 x 18g **LINDOR Milk Chocolate Eggs** (see Tip)

TO DECORATE:
Your choice of sugar sprinkles and edible decorations (you could also use freeze-dried raspberries or finely grated chocolate)

OR

Coloured royal icing or writing icing

1. Put the chopped chocolate into a heatproof bowl set over a pan of barely simmering water, ensuring the bottom of the bowl doesn't come into contact with the water, then stir until melted. Alternatively, pop the chocolate into a microwave-safe bowl and melt in 30-second bursts, stirring between each. Remove from the heat and leave to cool.

2. Carefully peel away the foil wrapper from the bottom of each egg to expose a small area of chocolate and gently insert a lollipop stick or small skewer, pushing halfway into the centre. Completely remove and discard the foil wrapper.

3. Gently dip the eggs into the cooled melted chocolate, swirling to coat completely. Lightly tap against the side of the bowl to remove any excess chocolate.

4. Hold over a plate (or sheet of greaseproof paper) and sprinkle with your choice of decorations. If using royal icing or writing icing, leave the chocolate coating to set (see next step) before piping on your chosen decorative pattern.

5. Carefully stand the pops in tall glasses or push the sticks through the holes of a colander or grater (taking care to ensure the pops do not touch each other) and leave until set. You can chill them in the fridge too but they may become more matte-looking.

CHOCOLATIER'S TIP
You can adapt this recipe and explore our range of LINDOR Truffles and Lindt EXCELLENCE Chocolate Bars to make different-flavoured pops throughout the year.

CHOCOLATE MISO PUMPKIN MARBLE CAKE

This beautiful loaf cake contains delicious giraffe-like swirls of intense chocolate, sweet and salty miso vanilla and vivid pumpkin. Light the fire, pour a mug of hot chocolate, snuggle under a blanket and enjoy a slice of this comforting autumnal bake. Thank you to @gourmetglow for this recipe.

SERVES: 8
PREP: 25 mins + chilling
COOK: 50 mins

115g unsalted butter,
    at room temperature,
    plus extra melted for
    greasing
150g plain flour, plus extra
    for dusting
200g caster sugar
2 large eggs
2 tsp baking powder
85g full-fat Greek yogurt
50g canned pumpkin purée
40g **Lindt EXCELLENCE
    70% Dark Chocolate**,
    melted (see Tip)
5g cocoa powder
½ tbsp white miso
½ tsp vanilla extract
1 tbsp icing sugar, for
    dusting

CHOCOLATIER'S TIP
For a more intense
chocolate flavour, try our
Lindt EXCELLENCE 85%
Dark Chocolate.

1. On the day, or a few hours before you want to make the cake, brush a 22 x 12 x 8cm fluted loaf tin with melted butter. Lightly dust with flour, shaking off any excess. Chill overnight or for a few hours – this helps achieve a more even bake.

2. Once the tin has chilled, preheat the oven to 170°C/150°C Fan/Gas 3.

3. Add the butter and sugar into the bowl of a stand mixer and beat on medium-high speed for 6–7 minutes, or until light and fluffy and all the sugar has dissolved.

4. Add the eggs, one at a time, beating well between each addition.

5. In a separate bowl, whisk together the flour and baking powder. With the beater running, add the flour in 2 additions, alternating with the yogurt. Take care not to overmix (a few lumps in the batter is fine, as it will be mixed again).

6. Weigh the batter and divide equally between 3 bowls.

7. Fold the pumpkin purée into one, the melted chocolate and cocoa powder into another, and the miso and vanilla extract into the third.

8. Spoon alternate mixtures into the tin so that no two colours are on top of each other, and keep adding until the tin is three-quarters full.

9. Tap the tin sharply 5 times on your work surface to even out the batters and release any air bubbles.

10. Bake for 40–50 minutes, or until a skewer inserted into the centre comes out clean.

11. Leave to cool in the tin for 10 minutes before turning out onto a wire rack to finish cooling completely. Add a dusting of icing sugar before serving.

MAPLE SYRUP CHOCOLATE SHARDS

These crunchy chocolate shards – made using our smooth EXCELLENCE Extra Creamy Milk Chocolate – are perfect for a homemade Christmas gift (if you can bear to share). Simply pop into cellophane bags and tie with pretty ribbons before handing out to friends and family (or sneaking into Christmas stockings).

SERVES: 10
PREP: 15 mins + chilling
COOK: 18 mins

115g unsalted butter,
 plus extra for greasing
150g caster sugar
175ml maple syrup
1 tsp vanilla extract
Pinch of salt
¼ tsp bicarbonate of soda
225g **Lindt EXCELLENCE Extra Creamy Milk Chocolate**, chopped (see Tip)
100g pecans, toasted and chopped (see Tip)

CHOCOLATIER'S TIP
For a more intense flavour, use our EXCELLENCE 70% Dark Chocolate. You can also try different nuts – chopped almonds, hazelnuts and macadamias work well.

1. Line a large baking sheet with greaseproof paper, ensuring there is enough overhang on all sides. Lightly grease with butter.

2. Add the sugar and maple syrup to a heavy-based saucepan. Add the butter, vanilla extract and salt. Bring to the boil over a medium-high heat, stirring occasionally, cooking until a sugar thermometer reads 146°C – watch carefully as the temperature rises rapidly from around 130°C. Immediately remove from the heat and carefully stir in the bicarbonate of soda.

3. Very carefully pour onto the prepared baking sheet and, using a spatula or palette knife, spread into an approximate 30 x 24cm rectangle. Leave to cool completely.

4. Meanwhile, put the chopped chocolate in a heatproof bowl set over a pan of barely simmering water, ensuring the bottom of the bowl doesn't come into contact with the water, then stir until melted. Alternatively, pop the chocolate into a microwave-safe bowl and melt in 30-second bursts, stirring between each. Remove from the heat and set aside to cool.

5. Once the maple slab has cooled, pour over half the melted chocolate and spread to cover. Sprinkle with half the chopped pecans. Chill for 15–20 minutes or until the chocolate has set.

6. Turn the slab over and peel off the greaseproof paper (you may need to use a piece of kitchen roll to remove the excess butter from the underside).

7. Pour over the remaining chocolate, spreading as before. Sprinkle with the remaining chopped pecans and chill for a further 15–20 minutes – or until completely set.

8. Break into pieces ready to put into cellophane bags (they will keep for up to 2 weeks in an airtight container) – or enjoy straight away!

CRUNCHY NUT CHRISTMAS BISCUITS

These delicious chocolate biscuits, topped with intense melted chocolate
and crunchy caramelised nuts, are perfect for pre-Christmas gatherings.

MAKES: 25–30
PREP: 40 mins + cooling
  and chilling
COOK: 20 mins

250g unsalted butter, diced
150g caster sugar
1 large egg
400g plain flour, plus extra
  for dusting
2 tbsp cocoa powder
Pinch of salt

TO DECORATE:
100g roasted salted
  peanuts
3 tbsp runny honey
2 tbsp water
Pinch of ground cinnamon
175g **Lindt EXCELLENCE
  70% Dark Chocolate**,
  chopped
Edible gold flakes
  (optional)

CHOCOLATIER'S TIP
You can get creative with
your cookie cutters and
create other festive shapes
such as stars and angels.

1. In an electric mixer, mix together the butter, sugar, egg, flour, cocoa powder and salt until you have a smooth dough. Wrap in cling film and chill in the fridge for about 1 hour.

2. Preheat the oven to 180°C/160°C Fan/Gas 4. Line a couple of baking sheets with greaseproof paper.

3. Roughly chop the peanuts and tip into a heatproof bowl.

4. Pour the honey into a frying pan with the water and cinnamon. Bring to the boil and simmer for 1–2 minutes until thick and golden. Add in the chopped peanuts, stir to coat, then cook for 1–2 minutes until sticky and the honey has reduced.

5. Tip onto a tray lined with baking paper and spread out in an even layer.

6. Lightly dust a work surface with flour before rolling out the dough to about 5mm thick. Stamp out Christmas tree-shaped cookies using a cookie cutter and transfer to the prepared baking sheets, leaving a couple of centimetres between each one.

7. Bake for about 12 minutes or until cooked. Leave to cool on the sheets for 5 minutes before using a palette knife to carefully transfer them to wire racks to finish cooling completely.

8. Meanwhile, put the chopped chocolate in a heatproof bowl set over a pan of barely simmering water, ensuring the bottom of the bowl doesn't come into contact with the water, then stir until melted. Alternatively, pop the chocolate into a microwave-safe bowl and melt in 30-second bursts, stirring between each. Remove from the heat and leave to cool for 15 minutes.

9. Brush the melted chocolate over the cooled cookies or dunk in the chocolate and tap off any excess. Sprinkle with the caramelised nuts and edible gold flakes, if using. Leave to set.

Photograph on p142

LINDT TEDDY CHOCOLATE CUPCAKES

Looking for a delicious Christmas bake for chocoholics? Discover these decadent chocolate cupcakes decorated with rich chocolate buttercream and a delicate milk chocolate Mini Lindt TEDDY.

MAKES: 12
PREP: 35 mins + cooling
COOK: 20 mins

FOR THE CUPCAKES:
90g plain flour
40g cocoa or cacao powder
1 tsp baking powder
½ tsp bicarbonate of soda
125ml buttermilk
80ml light olive oil
2 large eggs
130g caster sugar
30g soft light brown sugar

FOR THE FROSTING:
230g unsalted butter, at
　room temperature
300g icing sugar
40g cocoa or cacao powder
60ml double cream
12 x 10g **Mini Lindt
　TEDDY**, unwrapped
　(see Tip)

1. Preheat the oven to 180°C/160°C Fan/Gas 4. Line a 12-hole muffin tin with cases (see Tip).

2. In a medium-sized bowl, whisk together the flour, cocoa or cacao powder, baking powder and bicarbonate of soda and set aside.

3. In a large jug, whisk together the buttermilk, olive oil, eggs and sugars until combined.

4. Add the wet ingredients to the dry ingredients and whisk until just combined.

5. Pour the cake batter into your cupcake cases, filling them half to three-quarters full.

6. Bake in the oven for 18–20 minutes, or until well risen and the cake bounces back when gently touched. Leave to cool in the tins for 5 minutes, before transferring to a wire rack to finish cooling completely.

7. Meanwhile, prepare the frosting: in a large bowl, using an electric handheld mixer, beat the butter until smooth.

8. Sift in half of the icing sugar and the cocoa or cacao powder, then beat to combine. Sift in the remaining icing sugar and add the cream before beating until smooth.

9. When the cupcakes have completely cooled, spoon the frosting into a piping bag fitted with a star nozzle and pipe swirls onto the cupcakes. Top each cupcake with a Mini Lindt TEDDY and enjoy!

CHOCOLATIER'S TIP
This recipe is delicious throughout the year; try decorating with our 10g Mini Lindt GOLD BUNNY at Easter, red or pink cases and blissful LINDOR Truffles for Valentine's Day.

LINDOR PINWHEEL BISCUITS

Inspired by the classic Finnish pinwheel cookies, this recipe swaps
the traditional plum jam centre for an irresistible smooth LINDOR Truffle
surrounded by indulgent chocolate icing. With over 25 flavours of our
luxurious LINDOR Truffles to choose from,
you really are spoilt for choice!

MAKES: 30–36
PREP: 45 mins + cooling
and chilling
COOK: 15 mins

FOR THE BISCUITS:
225g unsalted butter,
 at room temperature
100g caster sugar
100g light brown sugar
250g full-fat cream
 cheese, at room
 temperature
1 large egg
1 tsp vanilla extract
390g plain flour, plus extra
 for dusting
Pinch of salt
2 tbsp milk
18 **LINDOR Truffles**
 (your choice of flavour),
 unwrapped and sliced in
 half (see Tip)

1. Place the butter and sugars in the bowl of a stand mixer (or use a large bowl with an electric hand mixer) and beat on medium-high speed until creamed together but not fluffy, scraping down the sides. Add the cream cheese, egg and vanilla extract. Beat on medium-high for 2 minutes or until light, fluffy and smooth.

2. In a separate bowl, whisk together the flour and salt. Tip into the butter mixture and mix on a low speed until the dough comes together. Don't overmix at this stage otherwise your biscuits will be tough.

3. Tip out the dough onto a flat surface lightly dusted with flour. Knead for a few minutes until it comes together to form a smooth dough. Divide into quarters, flatten into squares, wrap in cling film and chill for at least 2 hours (or overnight).

4. Preheat the oven to 180°C/160°C Fan/Gas 4 and line a couple of baking trays with baking paper.

5. Working with a quarter of your dough at a time, roll out the dough on a work surface lightly dusted with flour to 6mm thick to form a larger square. Using a knife, trim the edges to create straight sides. Cut each square into smaller 7.5 x 7.5-cm squares – use a cookie cutter if you have one. Transfer to the prepared baking trays, spaced at least 2.5cm apart. Chill for 10 minutes.

6. Working with 1 square at a time, make 2.5cm slits on each corner diagonally into the centre of the biscuit.

7. Brush the milk over the biscuits. Press the left side of every cut slit into the centre of the biscuit, pressing to seal and form a pinwheel. Brush the top with the milk. Chill for 15 minutes. Repeat with the remaining squares of dough, re-rolling any scraps.

FOR THE ICING:
50g **Lindt EXCELLENCE 70% Dark Chocolate**, chopped
115g unsalted butter, at room temperature
240g icing sugar
2 tbsp cocoa powder
2 tbsp double cream

8. Bake for 10–12 minutes or until just golden on the edges. You might need to do this in batches. Leave to cool on the baking tray for about 15 minutes before transferring to a wire rack to finish cooling completely.

9. While the biscuits are cooling, make the icing: put the chopped Lindt EXCELLENCE 70% Dark Chocolate in a heatproof bowl set over a pan of barely simmering water, ensuring the bottom of the bowl doesn't come into contact with the water, then stir until melted. Alternatively, pop the chocolate into a microwave-safe bowl and melt in 30-second bursts, stirring between each. Remove from the heat and set aside to cool.

10. Place the butter, icing sugar, cocoa powder and double cream into the bowl of a stand mixer (or use a large bowl with an electric hand mixer) and beat on low speed until combined. Scrape in the cooled melted chocolate. Beat on medium-high speed for 2–3 minutes or until fluffy.

11. Spoon into a piping bag fitted with a 6mm star nozzle. Squeeze a little icing into the centre of a biscuit. Top with half a LINDOR Truffle. Pipe more chocolate icing around the LINDOR Truffle, to decorate. Repeat with the remaining biscuits.

Photograph overleaf →

CHOCOLATIER'S TIP
Mix and match your favourite LINDOR flavours. Why not try our fabulously fruity Strawberries & Cream or our tantalisingly tropical Coconut? If you prefer an indulgent chocolate flavour, take a look at our 60% Dark Chocolate or beautifully balanced Milk & White.

ESPRESSO PECAN CHOCOLATE CHIP COOKIES

All too often, vegan recipes fall flat – they may involve too many obscure ingredients, complicated cooking methods or lack flavour. This delicious recipe proves that doesn't have to be the case! Thanks to our irresistible Lindt EXCELLENCE 70% Dark Chocolate, you can enjoy these pecan and chocolate chip cookies without compromising on taste, texture or time when you fancy a plant-based treat...

MAKES: 13–16
PREP: 20 mins
COOK: 10 mins

110ml light olive oil
45ml soya milk
½ tsp vanilla paste
200g caster sugar
225g plain flour
1 tsp baking powder
Pinch of salt
100g **Lindt EXCELLENCE 70% Dark Chocolate, chopped**
50g pecans, roughly chopped

1. Preheat the oven to 200°C/180°C Fan/Gas 6. Line 2 large flat baking trays with baking paper.

2. Whisk the oil, soya milk, vanilla and sugar together in a large bowl. Add in the plain flour, baking powder and salt and mix together until you have a soft dough. Stir in three-quarters of the chopped chocolate and all the pecans.

3. Roll the dough into 50g balls and press each down into a disc. Press the remaining chocolate and pecans on the top of the cookies.

4. Place the cookies onto the prepared trays a few centimetres apart, as they will spread slightly during cooking. Bake for 8–10 minutes, in batches if needed, until golden brown around the edges. Leave to cool completely.

CHOCOLATIER'S TIP
Instead of chilling them, you can freeze the balls of dough to bake at a later date and enjoy a freshly baked treat whenever that cookie craving strikes. Simply add 3–4 minutes to the baking time above.

LINDOR YULE LOG

Our twist on the classic Christmas yule log featuring sweet vanilla icing, a rich chocolate ganache and a delicate decoration of LINDOR Truffles.

SERVES: 8–10
**PREP: 45 mins + cooling
  and chilling**
COOK: 15 mins

Butter, for greasing
65g plain flour
25g cocoa powder
1 tsp baking powder
Pinch of salt
5 large eggs, separated
150g caster sugar
50g **Lindt EXCELLENCE
  70% Dark Chocolate**,
  melted and cooled
75g icing sugar

FOR THE VANILLA ICING:
175g unsalted butter,
  at room temperature
240g icing sugar
60ml double cream
1 tsp vanilla extract

FOR THE MILK
  CHOCOLATE GANACHE:
75ml double cream
100g **Lindt EXCELLENCE
  Extra Creamy Milk
  Chocolate**, finely
  chopped

Ingredients continued
overleaf →

1. Preheat the oven to 180°C/160°C Fan/Gas 4. Grease and line a 38 x 25cm Swiss roll tin with baking paper.

2. Sift together the flour, cocoa powder, baking powder and salt into a medium-sized mixing bowl; set aside.

3. Using an electric mixer, beat the egg yolks with 4 tablespoons of the caster sugar until pale and thickened, it will take about 3–4 minutes. Fold in the melted chocolate using a large metal spoon, trying to keep as much air in the mixture as possible.

4. In a separate bowl, using an electric whisk, whisk the egg whites with the remaining sugar until soft peaks form. It's important the bowl is very clean of any grease so the whites whip up nicely. Carefully fold the egg whites bit by bit into the egg yolk and chocolate mixture. Sprinkle the flour mixture over the top and fold in gently, again trying to keep in as much air as possible.

5. Spoon the batter evenly into the prepared tin and lightly smooth over the top. Bake for 10–12 minutes or until the top springs back when lightly touched.

6. Meanwhile, sift the icing sugar onto a large rectangle of greaseproof paper bigger than your Swiss roll tin. Once your cake is cooked and is out of the oven, run a thin knife around the edge of the cake to loosen from the sides of the tin and invert the cake onto the sheet of icing sugar.

7. Carefully peel off the baking paper used to line the tin. While the cake is still warm, starting at the short side, roll up the cake using the sugared greaseproof paper, into a log shape. Place seam side down onto a wire rack and leave to cool completely.

Method continued overleaf →

LINDOR YULE LOG *continued*

TO DECORATE:
1 tbsp icing sugar
150g **LINDOR Milk Truffles**, unwrapped (see Tip)

8. Meanwhile, for the vanilla icing, beat the butter with half of the icing sugar, then beat in the cream, vanilla extract and remaining icing sugar until fluffy. Cover with cling film and set aside until your cake is cool.

9. For the ganache: pour the cream into a saucepan and slowly bring to a simmer. Remove from the heat and add the chopped chocolate. Whisk until smooth, glossy and melted. Pour into a heatproof bowl and leave to cool until spreadable but not set; about 15 minutes at room temperature or 5 minutes in the fridge.

10. Unroll the cooled cake and spread evenly with the vanilla icing, leaving a border of a few centimetres around the edges. Reroll the cake and place onto a flat serving plate, seam side down.

11. Spread the thickened ganache over the top and down the sides. Chill for at least 1 hour. Run a fork along the top and sides to create a bark-like texture and dust with icing sugar. Cut half the LINDOR Truffles in half and the other half into quarters, before arranging on top of the log.

CHOCOLATIER'S TIP
You can use our decadent LINDOR Milk Truffles if you prefer. This is delicious served with fresh raspberries or raspberry coulis.

CARAMEL ICE CREAM HOT CHOCOLATE

Discover true indulgence with this rich and decadent hot chocolate topped with scoops of melting vanilla ice cream and lashings of rich chocolate sauce.

SERVES: 2
PREP: 5 mins
COOK: 10 mins

FOR THE CHOCOLATE
SAUCE:
100g **Lindt EXCELLENCE 70% Dark Chocolate**, chopped
120ml double cream

FOR THE HOT
CHOCOLATE:
500ml full-fat milk
A couple of drops of vanilla extract
75g **Lindt EXCELLENCE 70% Dark Chocolate**, chopped
50g **Lindt EXCELLENCE Dark Caramel and Sea Salt**, chopped

TO SERVE:
25g **Lindt EXCELLENCE Dark Caramel and Sea Salt**, melted and cooled
4 scoops of good-quality vanilla ice cream

1. For the sauce: put the chopped chocolate into a heatproof bowl and set aside.

2. Pour the cream into a small saucepan and bring to a simmer. Pour the hot cream over the chopped chocolate and whisk until smooth. Pour into a small jug.

3. For the hot chocolate: pour the milk into a saucepan, add a couple of drops of vanilla extract, and slowly bring to the boil. Remove from the heat and gently whisk in the chopped chocolates until melted.

4. Dip the rim of 2 tall heatproof glasses or mugs into the melted Lindt EXCELLENCE Dark Caramel and Sea Salt, turning to coat the rims. Divide the hot chocolate between the 2 glasses. Top each with 2 scoops of vanilla ice cream and drizzle generously with the chocolate sauce. Serve straight away.

CHOCOLATIER'S TIP
Make this extra chocolatey by using chocolate ice cream instead of vanilla. You can finely chop the remaining 25g Lindt EXCELLENCE Dark Caramel and Sea Salt and sprinkle on top before serving instead of dipping the rims of the glasses or mugs, if you prefer.

INDEX

ACKNOWLEDGEMENTS

We're delighted that you've chosen this Lindt chocolate cookbook, and we truly appreciate your support in our mission to enchant the world with chocolate.

As we continue to inspire the everyday indulgence in rich, delectable chocolate creations, your support means the world to us. Together, we're crafting a future where the art of chocolate-making becomes a beloved norm in every kitchen.

This delicious journey wouldn't be possible without the passion and dedication of everyone involved in the Lindt UK team.

Ebury Press, an imprint of Ebury Publishing
Penguin Random House UK
One Embassy Gardens, 8 Viaduct Gdns,
Nine Elms, London SW11 7BW

Ebury Press is part of the Penguin Random House group of companies whose addresses can be found at global.penguinrandomhouse.com

First published by Ebury Press in 2025

www.penguin.co.uk
www.lindt.co.uk

A CIP catalogue record for this book is available from the British Library

ISBN 9781529948707

Assistant Editor: Izzy Frost
Publishing Director: Elizabeth Bond
Design: Louise Evans
Production: Percie Bridgwater
Photography: Andrew Burton
Reprographics: Peter Pawsey
Food Stylists: Liberty Mendez and Lucy Cottle
Prop Stylist: Daisy Shayler-Webb

Printed and bound in Germany by Mohn Media GmbH

The authorised representative in the EEA is Penguin Random House Ireland, Morrison Chambers, 32 Nassau Street, Dublin D02 YH68.